out of the ashes

out of the ashes

THE TRUE STORY OF HOW ONE MAN TURNED TRAGEDY INTO A MESSAGE OF SAFETY

CHARLIE MORECRAFT

CENTER
STREET

New York Boston Nashville

Center Street
Hachette Book Group
1290 Avenue of the Americas,
New York, NY 10104

www.CenterStreet.com

Printed in the United States of America

RRD-C

First Edition: October 2012
10 9 8 7 6 5 4 3 2

Center Street is a division of Hachette Book Group, Inc.
The Center Street name and logo are trademarks of Hachette Book Group, Inc.

The Hachette Speakers Bureau provides a wide range of authors for speaking events. To find out more, go to www.HachetteSpeakersBureau.com or call (866) 376-6591.

The publisher is not responsible for websites (or their content) that are not owned by the publisher.

Library of Congress Cataloging-in-Publication Data

Morecraft, Charlie.
  Out of the ashes : the true story of how one man turned tragedy into a message of safety / Charlie Morecraft. — First edition.
      pages cm
  Summary: "Former Exxon operator Charlie Morecraft shares a cautionary tale of how life can change in an instant when people fail to take responsibility for their actions. Through his near-fatal experience he gives hope and helpful advice to others to stay safe at home and at work" —Provided by the publisher.
  ISBN 978-1-4555-0847-1 (hardcover) — ISBN 978-1-4555-0846-4 (trade paperback)
  1. Morecraft, Charlie. 2. Accidents—United States—Prevention. 3. Industrial safety—United States. 4. Chemical burns—Patients—Biography. 5. Chemical burns—Patients—Rehabilitation. 6. Exxon Mobil Corporation—Employees—Biography. 7. Industrial accidents—New Jersey—History—20th century. 8. Industrial accidents—United States—Case studies. I. Title.
  HV676.A2M67 2012
  363.17'91092—dc23
  [B]   2012027135

I would like to thank:

My wife, Janet, for all her love, support, and inspiration.

*Eileen Morecraft Gilanyi, who raised our two
beautiful daughters.*

*My daughters, Dana and Jennifer, for their love and
endurance in spite of the circumstances.*

*My mother, Nellie, and my father, Charlie, for never leaving
my side and giving me the will to live.*

*A special nurse, Roseanne Pona, who facilitated
my incredible care.*

contents

FOREWORD · *ix*

ACKNOWLEDGMENTS · *xv*

Prologue: Soul on Fire · *1*

Chapter 1: Safety Always · *5*

Chapter 2: Summer, Interrupted · *15*

Chapter 3: The Boxer's Pose · *27*

Chapter 4: Smoldering Embers—a Family in Denial · *57*

Chapter 5: How NOT to Be a Survivor · *79*

Chapter 6: My Definition of Safety · *107*

Chapter 7: Safety, It's Everyone's Responsibility · *123*

Chapter 8: Safety at Home · *149*

Chapter 9: Safety on the Road · *171*

Chapter 10: Safety on the Job · *187*

Chapter 11: The Nine Rules of Safety · *247*

Chapter 12: The Phoenix Rises · *267*

Epilogue: Everyone Deserves a Future (Even Elephants!) · *279*

ABOUT THE AUTHOR: CHARLIE MORECRAFT · *285*

foreword

THE CHARLIE MORECRAFT STORY:
IGNITING EMPOWERMENT FOR SAFETY

E. Scott Geller, Ph.D.
Alumni Distinguished Professor, Virginia Tech
Senior Partner, Safety Performance Solutions

Are you empowered for safety? I'm not asking whether you have authority over holding people accountable for complying with safety rules or regulations. And I'm not inquiring whether a supervisor has given you more responsibility for safety-related objectives. You know, "I empower you to get more done with fewer resources." These are management definitions of "empowerment."

I'm referring to the psychological definition of "empowerment." It's about "feeling empowered." When you feel empowered for safety you take personal responsibility for and ownership of safety. You are self-motivated to keep yourself and others safe. In this ideal state, you actively care for the health, safety, and welfare of others on a daily basis.

So how do you know whether you're empowered for safety? How can you determine whether certain colleagues feel empowered to prevent injuries to themselves and others? Psychological science provides an easy evidence-based technique for assessing empowerment. Simply ask yourself or someone else three yes/no questions. A "yes" answer to all three of these questions reflects empowerment, self-accountability, and self-motivation for safety.

First Question: Can you do it?

Can you accomplish the process or procedures you are asked to do for injury prevention? Do you have the resources, the time, the knowledge, skills, and ability to handle this responsibility? For occupational safety, this is essentially a training question. Have you been adequately trained to do the right things for safety within the environmental context in which you work? Thus, a "yes" to this question can usually be obtained with proper instruction and allocation of resources.

Second Question: Will it work?

Do you believe the process or procedures you are asked to do for safety will be effective in preventing injuries? People might feel competent at conducting interpersonal observation and feedback, but not believe a coaching process can work to decrease overall injury rate. They could believe, for example, workers will only role-play safe behavior when they know they're being observed, but revert to their routine at-risk behavior when the observer leaves.

Third Question: Is it worth it?

People can be trained to feel competent at executing a safety-related program, and believe the techniques will work to prevent injuries, but not be motivated to perform. For example, it's easy to avoid text-messaging and talking on a cell phone while driving. In addition to common sense, there's indisputable evidence many vehicle crashes and fatalities would be prevented if drivers stopped using their cell phones while driving. Yet, so many drivers perform this unsafe behavior. Why? Because like so many risky behaviors, people are not sufficiently motivated to change. The soon, certain, and positive consequences of using "windshield time" to communicate via cell phone are powerful and extremely difficult to overcome.

The Motivation Challenge. Motivating human behavior for safety is always a challenge, because safety-related behaviors are relatively inconvenient, time consuming, and sometimes uncomfortable. Plus, the natural supportive consequences of safety-related behaviors are neither soon nor certain, but rather delayed and uncertain. It's human nature to believe, "I can take risks because something bad won't happen to me," and it usually doesn't. Risky behaviors like speeding in a vehicle, taking a procedural shortcut, and text-messaging or talking on a cell phone while driving are followed by soon and certain positive consequences like comfort, convenience, and/or saving time. Then, natural ongoing consequences reinforce and maintain these at-risk behaviors.

The three E-words of traditional safety—Engineering, Education, and Enforcement—and their concomitant intervention strategies are not sufficient to activate and sustain human involvement in safety-related activities. Three additional E-words require our attention—Empowerment, Empathy, and Emotion. These are exemplified in Charlie Morecraft's autobiographical story, as he has told it to over half a million people in over fifteen different countries, including every branch of the U.S. Military, and as it's shared in this provocative book.

From Empathy to Emotion. Charlie Morecraft is the most effective motivational communicator I've observed in over forty years of attending regional and national safety conferences. I've heard Charlie reveal his riveting personal story on more than twenty occasions, and every time he motivates me to feel more empowered for safety. His energizing and passionate delivery engages every audience member to feel empathy for him throughout vivid descriptions of his heartrending experiences preceding and following one hot August night in 1980 when his risky behavior ignited a horrific "fire hurricane" that almost blew up an entire Exxon oil refinery. Then come the emotions. There's not a dry eye in the auditorium as Charlie describes the disastrous and dismal consequences of this tragedy, from the horrendous pain he endured to the psychological trauma inflicted on his family.

A few years ago, while Charlie was addressing the five hundred attendees of a people-based safety conference sponsored by Safety Performance Solutions (a consulting firm I co-founded), an audience member fainted and rolled off his chair to the floor. While this man received appropriate attention, I walked to the stage and asked Charlie, "Are you okay?" "Oh, yes," he said. "He'll be fine; I've seen this happen more than two hundred times, and it's always a male, never a female." I later asked this individual what happened, and he said, "I'm not sure; I got so into Charlie's descriptions of his painful ordeals at the burn-treatment center that I imagined it happening to me. That's all I remember."

I've never seen a speaker bring emotions of genuine caring out of people like Charlie Morecraft does. Emotions are motivating. Safety-related emotions, which you will surely sense when reading this book, arouse an empathic "yes" answer to the question, "Is it worth it?"

In Conclusion

The empowerment needed for people to actively care for safety when no one's watching requires more than training, education, and enforcement. People need to believe all the extra inconvenient behaviors called for to sustain an injury-free culture are worth the effort. Group statistics do not foster this belief. This belief happens when people make safety a personal value. This will happen when you empathize with Charlie Morecraft's story and are touched with emotion when visualizing the intolerable short- and long-term consequences he endured.

You will realize something like that can happen to you if you continue to choose convenient and time-saving at-risk behavior over more inconvenient and effortful safe behavior. Reading this book will activate personal empathy and emotion and enable you to feel empowered for safety.

acknowledgments

I would like to thank St. Barnabas Hospital for their incredible care. I'd also like to thank Rusty Fischer for his dedication and help in writing this book. In memoriam, I'd like to acknowledge Eileen, the mother of my two beautiful daughters—she raised them well.

out of the ashes

Prologue

There was a moment there, just before I took that final step, where time slowed to a crawl. I could almost hear the movie of my life screeching to a halt as time hit the big "pause" button in the sky; it sounded like a needle scratching across one of my old 45-records.

I could see everything as if I was watching it from outside myself. I could see the gushing chemicals at my back, the fallen tools, even my wet footprints as I stumbled blindly down from the pipeline joint.

I could smell the chemicals that doused my body, the way they were already reacting with my vulnerable skin, my exposed arms and neck, my ears and face. I was covered in it, I could taste it, bitter on my tongue and stinging my gums.

I could feel it seeping into my pores.

I could barely see two steps in front of me, but I could see all that in my mind's eye. I knew what was happening; my worst nightmare. I knew I was in it now, and that every step forward meant survival, every second wasted meant I was just one step closer to death.

I was already dying by inches. These chemicals were nothing to fool with. Every second of exposure, every moment they lingered on my skin, in my eyes, up my nose, seeping through my clothes, could be life threatening.

I had decided, in the moments just after the spill, eyes blinded by the exposure, skin searing with the sting, that if I could just make it to the chemical shower a few yards away, I'd be okay; I'd at least survive. The gushing water would get rid of most of it, the skeleton crew at the local ER could deal with the rest.

I might lose an eye, I might lose my hearing, my sense of taste, I might even look like crap for the rest of my life, but I'd live to tell the story at some smoky dive bar and that would be enough.

There was nothing standing in my way of making it to that shower. Nothing, that is, but my truck. My running truck. All the rules I'd broken that night, all the policies and procedures I'd ignored—the rolled-up sleeves, the no hard hat, the missing safety goggles and the heavy gloves I hadn't worn because they were too bulky and slow—all of that paled in comparison to that truck sitting there between me and the safety shower.

To the average citizen, a running vehicle is a convenience, something you leave in "park" when running into the corner store for a gallon of milk or zipping inside the daycare to pick up your kid on the way home from work.

At a chemical refinery, it's an ignition source. No different from a lighter or a book of matches or a Roman candle. We're taught from day one on the job, from minute one practically, never to leave the truck running out on the line. And there it was, rumbling away, the exhaust pluming into the air from the trembling tailpipe. And there I was, dripping from head to toe with just about the most highly flammable chemicals on the planet, screaming (probably) from the pain, about to step right into its path.

In that second of realization, in that slowed down moment of perfect and utterly useless clarity, I saw it all happen but was powerless to stop it. It was too late to back up and go around the truck. It was too late to back up at all. I plunged ahead, boots heavy and slick and wet, momentum carrying me forward and my worst fears were realized: in an instant, I was consumed in fire.

It was too hot to feel, it was too sudden to hurt. At that moment I was every bad actor you've ever seen in every bad, B–horror movie, flailing around with my head, my arms, my torso, my legs covered in flame. Only there was no stunt coordinator just out of range, waiting and ready with a heavy fireproof blanket and an industrial grade fire extinguisher to put me out when the director yelled "Cut!"

I was underwater with a wave of flames swirling around me, disoriented and turned around. I stumbled left, then right, then back again in circles, while every second my skin was falling prey to the hungry fire. And that was when I knew I wouldn't reach the chemical shower.

I'd be dead by then.

Who knows, I might even be dead already…

CHAPTER 1

Safety Always

My name is Charlie Morecraft, and once upon a time, I used to work for Exxon. I worked for them for nearly thirty years off and on. And I'm not just talking about sitting in some corner office somewhere, pushing papers around my desk all day.

I'm talking the low-down, dirty, don't-talk-about-it-in-polite-company jobs. You name an Exxon job, I've most likely done it. Digging ditches in the stinging rain, docking delivery barges at 4:00 a.m. in the driving snow, walking the line, working the line, and finally, managing the line—that was me.

That was my life, and the Exxon refinery was my home. I mean that almost literally; I lived about ten minutes away from the plant. It seemed like as soon as I got home from one shift, I was turning around a few hours later and heading back to work.

The crazy thing is after all that's happened between us, I

still retain Exxon as a client to this day. A very good client, in fact. I speak to their safety supervisors, and consult on new safety initiatives. They gave me my first speaking gig, and I still speak to their employees frequently.

Exxon's been very, very good to me.

Hell, they kept me on even after I blew myself up, blew up that truck, and did millions of dollars of damage to the refinery where I worked. I even got a promotion when I came back!

That's right, to "safety manager" of all things.

But wait; I'm getting a little ahead of myself. Before that fateful night, I was what they called an "oil movement operator" at Exxon. Basically, I worked out in the field, blending the gasoline that gushed through the refinery in miles-long pipelines that snaked throughout the sprawling plant near Linden, New Jersey.

For those of you who can't picture Linden, New Jersey, or, for that matter, an oil refinery plant, think of the opening credits of the hit HBO series *The Sopranos*. You know the one, with Tony driving in his big SUV down the turnpike—arm out the window, big fat stogie in his mouth—and those three or four dingy, white dome-type buildings passing by on the side of the road. That's where I worked, day in, day out, for nearly thirty years.

Until my careless ways caught up with me, that is.

So that was me: dutiful, dependable, lived right down the road, always up for a double shift, knew what I was doing, and wasn't shy about telling others how to do their job while I was at it.

But I was on the line and not in the office, and that meant a lot in those days. Me and the guys I worked with, most of us, talked tough, lived hard, and drank harder. We were guys' guys because only the toughest of the tough could do what we did—and survive.

I was also the guy who always thought that safety meetings were for catching up on my sleep in the back of the room, that safety equipment was for wusses, and that if you knew your job, you could take shortcuts without any problem.

Accidents were for other people, clowns mostly. Wusses, punks. Guys who couldn't handle their business or their liquor or were never meant for this line of work in the first place. I absolutely believed that an accident would never happen to me—ever.

And even if it did, I reasoned, the only one who would be hurt by it would be me alone. Not my kids, my parents, or my friends. Not my colleagues at the refinery or my bosses or the other guys who counted on me to lead by example.

I believed all of this until the night of August 8, 1980, when I took a ten-minute shortcut that would take the next thirty years to recover from. Who am I kidding?

I'm still in recovery to this day.

Sunglasses and Safety Meetings

To put it mildly, I was never, ever overly concerned about safety on the job. Not my first year, not after fifteen years, and certainly not after nearly thirty years.

To me, safety meetings—what a joke!—were nothing but glorified pep talks, dog and pony shows that management put on because, frankly, they had to.

Truth be told, if I knew ahead of time we were having a safety meeting I'd be sure to get good and hammered the night before. After all, what better way to sleep off a bender—and get paid for it—than during one of these snooze fests?

Back then if you walked into one of our safety meetings, you would have been able to spot me right off: I'd be the guy in the back, slouched down so no one would call on me, black sunglasses on in the middle of the day so none of the supervisors could tell if I was sleeping or not. (And I usually was.)

At our refinery, they'd put up a list before every meeting of how many accidents we'd had at the plant over the past year. This was very serious stuff. You've probably seen a list like this. You know, how many first aid injuries, how many disabling injuries, how many reportable injuries, that kind of thing.

And while everybody else sat there and nodded their heads very somberly, pledging to do better next time, I'd always think to myself, *Well, what do you expect? It's a chemical plant. I mean, if you're going to run a place like this, you're going to have accidents. It's part of the job; it's inevitable. No matter what all those experts say, accidents happen, and no, they're not preventable.*

My attitude about working was the same as my attitude about drinking: live fast, die hard, and leave behind a pretty corpse. I figured if drinking didn't kill me, the plant would or vice versa. Either way I was pretty much toast, so to speak, so why bother worrying about it too much?

Frankly, I didn't worry about too much back then, period. I didn't let the fact that I had a wife at home, two beautiful daughters, or bills and responsibilities slow me down any. I worked hard, I played hard, and I saw my family on weekends and the holidays. Like everybody else, right?

That's how it was back then; that's how we all did it. The wives understood, the kids figured it was just a way of life, and we line guys didn't care much either way.

It's a Win-Win

By this point I'd been working the same job for fifteen years. Five or six shifts a week, fifty or so weeks a year, every year like clockwork. So I knew the job upside down and inside out, back to front, and around the side. I'd come to expect a bump here or a bruise there or maybe a stitch or two in the line of duty, but nothing *that* bad.

I even knew other operators who had been hurt on the job, and it was nothing I couldn't handle. In fact, getting hurt on the job was kind of a "win-win" situation, if you ask me. Case in point: I'll never forget the day I went out on the line with my supervisor, Pete.

Whatever job it was we were doing that day, Pete tried jumping over a load of pipes, misjudged the angle, and promptly tripped. As I watched Pete lose his balance in the slow-motion capture, I thought to myself, *This isn't going to end well*. I was right. When Pete came down—hard—he fractured his ankle.

Big deal. The hospital sent him home with one of those sissy casts—you know, the kind you can walk around on—and he got three months off with pay. I said it: with pay! Not only that, but he came out ahead on the deal when compensation awarded him an extra $2,000 for his trouble.

What trouble? A cast he could wear to Giants Stadium and an extra two grand for beer money? If that's trouble, sign me up! Besides, you and I both know old Pete only needed about a month off before his ankle was well enough for him to get back to work. After that, he was in the catbird seat for those extra two months. Plus he got his full pay the whole time he was out, so the extra two grand probably went to pay off his aboveground pool. Where's the harm in all that?

I thought, *Wow, if that's the worst that's going to happen to me on the job, I can deal with that!*

To me, management always spoke two languages. There was "corporate speak," which sounded a lot like what was printed in the company brochure and how the guy who interviewed me for the job talked.

Corporate speak sounded a lot like this: "To rectify the poor safety percentages at this plant, we're going to usher in a new era of paradigm shift that will encompass several new initiatives designed to streamline performance while also serving to maintain the proper corporate culture in an effort to maximize yada yada yada…"

And then there was "line speak," or what really happened, day in, day out, when you were suited up and had a wrench in your hand. Line speak sounded more like this: "Look, guys, today we've finally got to clean out that beast of a tank out on Lot Eight. So, who's not hungover today? Okay, Lucky, you take Bruiser and..."

As for myself, I was more concerned with expediency than safety. If I never made it to plant supervisor, fine by me. I already made good money on the line doing what I did so I wasn't hurting for dough, and I was hardly what you'd call ambitious back then.

My family was cared for, I knew the job, lived close to the plant, the girls went to good schools...life was good. All I wanted was to do my job as quickly and painlessly as possible so I could hit Murphy's Pub before last call. If that meant I had to bypass a few safety protocols to get the job done quicker and sooner, then so be it.

It was my call, and most days, that's how I chose to make it. Getting the job done, for me, was the bottom line. How you got it done? Well, the end justified the means as far as I was concerned back then.

We're Number Two!

From the day I got my first time card to today, Exxon has always, *always* said that safety was their number one priority. But I always figured, well, what were they gonna say? "We're number two?!?" How would that look on their business cards, you know?

I figured they got a tax break for saying stuff like that, that their safety meetings and "days without incident" reports got them some kind of a sweet bonus from safety organizations, that the government subsidized those meetings—or even that slogan.

I also figured that if push came to shove, if production slowed or profits suffered because of overdue safety concerns—well, that I was supposed to read between the lines and recognize that safety really *was* second and profits were first.

The fact was safety did come first to Exxon—then, now, and always. It just didn't come first to some of their workers, namely, me. Well, me and Pete that is.

The Dynamic Duo

You remember Pete, don't you? Mr. Sissy Cast and Three Months Off Plus a Two-Grand Bonus? Well, one of the reasons management was so good to Pete while he was out on injury is because, like me, Pete wasn't afraid to get his hands dirty. In fact, you could say that old Pete and I specialized in dirty deeds (not necessarily) done dirt cheap.

If management needed something done yesterday, they gave it to me and my partner, Pete. They called us the dynamic duo because we'd take any comers, no matter how big, ugly, or dirty the job was.

We handled what guys called the "hot jobs." Jobs that

weren't necessarily by the book. Ugly jobs, unsafe jobs, jobs most other guys wouldn't touch.

Like me, Pete enjoyed his alcohol. Maybe both of us enjoyed it a little too much at times, but so far so good. We'd gotten away with it all these years, what was to stop us now?

And besides, we never, ever, *ever* drank on the job. That was rule number one. Rule number two was pretty much everything else goes, good, bad, or in between.

That's why we got all the tough jobs, the dirty jobs, the hush-hush jobs management couldn't trust to the rest of the Dudley Do-Rights on the floor. We both figured if we hadn't died from drinking as much as we did, hell, no *way* were we going to die on the job.

So we were kind of like the plant daredevils. We got things done fast because we bypassed safety procedures. Night or day, weekend or holiday, you could always count on the dynamic duo to get the job done fast, if not safely.

Looking back, Pete and I were kind of the plant outlaws. I didn't notice it at the time because, well, it wasn't like the rest of the guys were shrinking violets either, you know? I mean, we weren't exactly Hells Angels at a debutante ball, if you get my drift.

Look, chemical plants—pretty much any hazardous job, really—are rough-and-tumble places. You kind of have to be a little bit of an outlaw to work in one. Maybe not upstairs in the corner office or in human resources or at the front desk or as a sales rep, but if you wore a hard hat or a tool belt or drove a pickup truck to work, well, you fit right in.

But what I never realized back then was that even in the Wild West, some outlaws were wilder than others. At Exxon, I was wilder than most, wilder, certainly, than was good for me or my coworkers.

And like the gunslingers of old, I was headed for a deadly showdown that would prove who was boss. Unlike those gun-toting tough guys, however, my showdown was with the fiercest opponent of all: myself.

CHAPTER 2

Summer, Interrupted

My family and I were due to start our summer vacation on the Jersey shore any minute now. We'd rented a bungalow on the beach, in fact, and my wife and two daughters were already waiting for me there.

I could picture them there, unpacking or maybe snacking on cheese and crackers, feet in the sand, the sound of the waves crashing, waiting for their old man to get off work. And my mouth was positively watering for the big cooler full of beer my wife would have waiting for me, a frosty one ripe and ready to go. I could almost taste it.

Seems like my family was always waiting for me to get off work, but pretty soon now I'd be with them and we'd have two glorious weeks to catch up as summer ended and fall began.

My daughters were as different as night and day. I know lots of fathers say that, but in my case, it was fact. There was Jennifer, the youngest, as outgoing and boisterous as her old man. She'd never met a stranger, which as a father sometimes bothered me, but to know her was to love her and she never left a house sadder than when she entered.

I could picture her now, dragging her older sister, Dana, out of some hidey-hole, where she'd already started reading a book, and onto the soft white sand of the Jersey shore.

Dana, my oldest, was a quiet and sensitive soul but a beautiful girl who gave her heart fully to anyone she let inside. Once you were in Dana's circle, you were in for life; that was just how she was.

Together my two girls managed to be both loyal sisters and friends to each other and free spirits, fully independent of one another. It worked for them, and whenever we all got together like this, we jelled as few families do. So I was picturing my family as my shift wound down that night, eager to join them at the shore and start our summer vacation in earnest.

The Double Shift from Hell

It was a hot August night, and I was nearing the end of my 3 to 11 shift. Not surprisingly, my supervisor asked me if I'd work over, stay on to cover the 11 to 7 shift. I wasn't the only one taking vacation time lately, and August was a big month for double shifts.

In a way, I was kind of glad my latest trainee, Art, hadn't shown up that night. I liked Art; he was a good guy and I was training him in all the old "Cool Charlie" ways.

You know, "faster is better," "why take the long way when you can take a shortcut," that kind of thing. But Art was an older man, and if it was going to be someone holding the line on that hot August night, it was better to be a guy like me who'd done it a thousand times before. Let Art catch up on his beauty rest, and I'd catch up with him after my trip.

And me? Sure, I was eager to start my vacation, but I figured, *Why not?* I mean, think about it: at that time of night, there'd be no big bosses around to bust my chops, you know?

This way I could keep my head down, do my job, do it as quickly as possible, coast along until quitting time, head down to the beach, snooze on the shore with my wife and kids and a bucket of beer. What the hell, right? I'd even have a little overtime pay waiting in the bank to help with the vacation. Maybe I could use it to treat the family to a surprise lobster dinner once the check cleared!

Of course, life rarely goes as planned. Lo and behold, about an hour into my second shift I was back in the control house minding my own business, sitting with my feet up on the desk, when I got a call to go out to one of the refinery manifolds and change out one of the hammer blanks.

For those of you scratching your heads right now, a hammer blank is the joint where a pipeline comes together in a refinery. When it comes time to switch out a hammer blank, that means you either insert a solid piece of metal to stop the flow of hydrocarbon through the line or you pull it out to start the flow.

Imagine you're washing your car and you're halfway down the drive and don't want to walk all the way back to the faucet to turn it off. To stop the flow of water without doing all the legwork, you can simply fold the hose in two, and boom, instant water stoppage.

To release the flow, you just unfold the hose and you're back in business. Pipelines work in much the same fashion; it's all about regulating—stopping or starting—the flow of materials. (Congratulations, you've just passed Hammer Blank 101!)

In laymen's terms, my supervisor wanted me to go out to this manifold joint and pull out one of these blanks. Sounds complicated, maybe a little dicey? But for me, no worries. I'm not exaggerating when I say that I had literally done this job thousands of times before. It was nothing new to me, an everyday job.

Did I want to do it at the beginning of a double shift? Not really. It was a dirty, thankless, rather physical job, and after all, I'd been looking forward to coasting through the evening.

Truth be told, my mind was pretty much already on vacation, so was my body. And this was going to be a beast of a job, no doubt. These were older valves, so they would often get stuck in place, making them harder to open and close. Many was the time I had to go back to my work truck and haul out one of my monster wrenches to help seal one off or open one up.

We always complained about the job because regardless of how many times we'd done it, the valves always, always leaked whenever we had to head out there and switch out one of these blanks. It was such a sticking point that management was always going to change out these manifolds because they were older and problematic, but it never got done.

Plus it would have been a costly procedure and a capital outlay that would have meant a serious ding to our department's budget. So instead management implemented a safety procedure that would both reduce leaks and increase one's safety while working the job. It would also make a simple yank-and-pull job a half-shift procedure that was way too long if you followed protocol.

As far as I was concerned, doing it the right way was also the slow way. I had a nap to take, and I wasn't going to let work get in the way! Seriously, though, procedure meant that you were supposed to close two valves to remove the blank safely, one on either side of the flange that existed around the blank. One valve? No problem. Two valves? Well, that was ten minutes of extra work that I just wasn't patient enough for.

Tough Guy Takes a Fall

I was Charlie Morecraft, king of the swift and speedy. Mr. Sunglasses in Safety Meetings. Mr. Nothing's Going to Happen to Me. So I hopped in my truck and headed out to the manifold, quick as you please.

It was late that night, nearing midnight, and the dark

sky was lit by thousands of orange bulbs that stretched the length of the fence line, the pipeline, and the scaffolding that was everywhere you looked. It might have looked eerie to the odd civilian or passerby, the setting of some low-rent zombie movie, but to me it was my home away from home.

I barely noticed the billowing clouds of exhaust that stretched upward into the inky black night. I did notice the sticky August humidity and was glad that I was in my trademark muscle shirt.

If you've ever worn flame-retardant clothing, which was my standard uniform for the Exxon plant, you'd know it's heavy, it's sticky, it's thick, it's hot, and it's damn uncomfortable. So I had a simple solution: roll the sleeves up. No problem. Were your arms protected? Hell no, but you felt about ten degrees cooler that way, and at the time, that's pretty much all I cared about.

I was glad I'd rolled up my sleeves that night as I parked at the site, my bare arm slung over the open window of my truck. I thought briefly of turning the engine off, but why bother? I'd make quick work of switching out the hammer blank, hop back in my truck, and be back in time for some of the fresh coffee in the breakroom. Who knows, maybe by now one of the guys from the next shift would have brought doughnuts.

Safety goggles hung from the rearview mirror, but I ignored those as well. They fogged up on nights like this, cut off rather than assisted my vision, and like the sleeves of my shirt were uncomfortable. I left them behind. No worries.

The few metal steps boomed under my heavy work boots

as I walked onto the cramped platform. It felt as familiar to me as my front doorstep, the workbench in my two-car garage, or my back porch. Without much preamble, I put down my toolbox, bent to the manifold, and got to work.

Now, the proper procedure for this kind of operation was slow and laborious, almost painstaking. It was also the way "they" wanted us to do it—you know, management? Otherwise known as "the enemy." But I was from the "us versus them" school of thought, so if they wanted it done a certain way, I knew it had to be wrong or at least slow and unrealistic and designed to test our patience at every turn.

Those guys, in their shirts and ties, they'd never been on the line. Or if they had, it had been so long ago they'd forgotten what it was like in the trenches, wrench in hand, trying to understand—let alone implement—their lengthy procedures. They didn't know or remember what it was like to follow procedure when that meant sweat dripping in your eyes, tearing off a fingernail or two trying to get a rusty valve open in the middle of the night. Naw, better to do it my way, the right way. Or if not right, then at least quick.

For those of you who've never worked in a refinery before, I'll try to set up the scene. When two pieces of pipeline come together, they do so at a flange, or joint. It's no different than when two pieces of pipe, say, behind your toilet or under your kitchen sink, come together. Same concept, just on a little—okay, a lot—bigger scale.

Whenever you do work on this intersection, you're supposed to close the two valves on either side of the flange. This way if one of the valves fails, the other one holds and you're not exposed to a rushing gush of toxic chemicals that could quickly destroy your life.

Well, that night, I only closed one valve. The reason I didn't close the other one was because it was one tough valve. We're talking a pain in the butt to close, and frankly, I wasn't up for it. But what's more, I'd always gotten away with just closing the one valve before.

Of course, if I'd followed proper procedure I could have avoided 100 percent of the risk I was exposing myself to that night, but I'd done this plenty of times before and my heart rate wasn't rising. Besides, this way I'd save myself a good ten minutes. Imagine that; ten minutes that would have changed the rest of my life. But I wasn't thinking about my life at the time, just living it to the hilt.

I'd be fine. I always was. Remember, I'd done this a thousand times before. The leaks, small at first, started right away as I knew they would. No big deal. Pipes this old, valves this rusty, you're gonna expect some leaks; it comes with the territory.

What was leaking was a chemical additive called isomerate, or ISOM feed. It's basically an octane enhancer to give the gasoline an extra boost to go from unleaded to unleaded extra. So if you're the kind who pays an extra ten cents or so at the pump for the good stuff, now you at least know what your money's getting you: ISOM feed.

Now, at Exxon, there was a contingency for every contingency, a backup for every backup. In the case of this particular flange, the leaks were designed to feed into a long trough down below, and with each step of the procedure, there was a little more runoff building up in the trough. Just one more reason to hurry up and get off this pipeline faster than slower.

Then the leaks got a little bigger. But I was still okay; this kind of leakage was acceptable. Remember, I'd done this a hundred, a thousand times before. I'd be all right.

Finally, the leak subsided to where I felt it was safe to finally hoist the hammer blank up and out of the manifold. You know, the original job I was actually there to do? And then, as if out of nowhere, a huge surge of chemical rushed up and over the manifold surface straight onto my face and gushing down my chest.

I often wonder to this day if I'd been wearing my safety glasses would I have made it out of there in one piece? At that point, vision was critical. If I could have seen where I was going, spotted the chemical shower sooner, avoided the truck in my path, who knows? Maybe I'd be writing a very different book right now, if at all. I guess we'll never know. Safety glasses weren't cool, remember. I never wore them.

Instead I stumbled around, temporarily blinded by the stinging chemicals that had splashed up into my eyes. Still, my training took over, and if ever there was a workplace accident, this certainly qualified. Not only was I covered in a toxic chemical, but the blank was half up, half down, and now that same chemical was gushing like a geyser from the pipeline.

I had to get help, had to stop this flow, had to get control of this situation before it got out of hand. But to do all that, first I had to see what the hell I was doing! The shower.

Somehow I knew if I could just make it to the shower, I'd be fine.

Maybe not "fine," but I'd live; I'd survive, at least.

That was my only goal at the moment: survival.

Forget the wife and kids waiting in the rental cottage by the sea, forget the hazardous chemicals still gushing from the manifold at my back, forget the demotion I'd probably get from screwing up royally. (That is, if Exxon let me keep my job in the first place.)

Just let me survive, Lord; I'll take it from there.

I could barely see as I stumbled forward, praying for my life. The gushing chemical covering my face, my neck, my ears, my upper torso, my arms, my thick work gloves.

As I never wore safety goggles, I was temporarily blinded so the images that surrounded me—hazy streetlights, the security fence, rickety scaffolding, and miles of pipeline— were blurry at best as I stumbled from the manifold, down the slick metal steps, and hit the ground running.

As the chemical stung my eyes and gravel crunched under my saturated work boots, I knew there was a safety shower a block or two away.

Now, if I could just get there.

This much I knew: the shower meant survival.

I ran, I bolted, pawing at my eyes, stumbling forward, knowing every minute that the ISOM covered me I risked losing my vision, my sense of smell, my hearing, even my voice.

Time stood still even though I knew everything was happening very, very quickly.

I could feel the chemical soaking through my Nomex fireproof clothing, I could taste it on my tongue as if I'd just tried to siphon fuel out of the world's biggest gas tank, and I could hear my feet stumbling forward, heavy work boots slapping tiny puddles from the late summer thunderstorms we'd been having lately.

That wasn't the only sound I heard.

There was a motor running somewhere nearby, *my* motor.

As I stumbled toward the shower, I could literally see the fuel vapors rising off of me the way you can see heat shimmering off asphalt on a hot summer day.

Suddenly, that sight made me sick to my core. It wasn't the vapors themselves that had me suddenly queasy, but what they represented: fire.

I'd left my work truck running, and I could see the vapor cloud surrounding me, an open invitation to ignite on impact.

I ran past the truck at the same time I saw the fumes drifting toward it.

There's a rule in the refinery that says you never, ever leave your truck or vehicle running because it could become an ignition source. In other words, a running truck is pretty much the workplace equivalent of smoking at the gas pump. Like the safety goggles, though, that was just one more safety procedure I never quite followed.

Why bother? It was inconvenient, a real pain in the ass. I was always jumping in and out of my truck to do a quick job anyway. And as I ran past the truck that night, blindly groping for the safety shower, I knew what was going to happen.

I could see it coming.

I could feel it coming.

I was powerless to stop it.

The vapors, the ISOM, the running exhaust pipe, the physics of it all—there was no way to avoid it.

My entire body ignited instantly.

I just kept running, stumbling blindly toward that chemical shower.

It was like one of those scenes you see in the movies: a flaming man stumbling forward, screaming silently as flames sear his lungs, arms waving wildly, flaming clothes dripping from his skin.

It didn't hurt... at first.

It was still too early for the pain. Maybe I was in shock, maybe my nerve endings had already been burned off, or maybe I'd never feel anything ever again.

All I knew at that moment was that I wouldn't make it to the shower in time. It was too far; I'd be walking charcoal by then. Hell, I was practically that now.

Somehow out of the corner of my eye, I saw a puddle of standing water sitting under a stack of runoff pipes. *Please, God, let it be water and not more fuel!* I took a chance that it was water and not more fuel and threw myself into it to douse the flames.

For once, I caught a break. It *was* water; I was no longer on fire.

Unfortunately, my night was just beginning...

CHAPTER 3

The Boxer's Pose

Somehow I stood on wobbly legs, a lone figure in the midst of a raging inferno that used to be a refinery. I reached for my radio to call in help, but it wasn't there on my belt where I always kept it. Like half my clothes, it had been blown off in the explosion.

In *my* explosion, in the explosion that was me.

Amazingly, I felt no pain. You would think you'd lose consciousness at a moment like that, half your body burned, lungs singed, lips melted, blind in one eye, deaf in one ear. Instead, my training kicked in as I tried to run around shutting off valves to contain the fire that had resulted when I bolted past my running truck.

I could only imagine what I looked like at that point, half-naked, clothes literally blown off, running around checking fire gauges and turning off valves, barely able to see and not knowing what I was looking at in the first place. I was literally in the eye of a fire hurricane. Everything around me was on fire, everything but me. At least I'd managed to put myself out first, if nothing else.

And I can clearly remember thinking that my biggest concern at the time, frankly my only concern at the time, was this: *Look at this place! Half the damn refinery's on fire! They're going to fire me for sure when they get a load of this!*

When I say it seemed like it took forever for the fire crews and emergency vehicles to get to me, I'm not exaggerating; it did take longer than usual. That's because they literally had to fight their way through the burning refinery inferno to get to me.

The first guy through the "fire line," as it were, was a good friend of mine, still is a good friend of mine to this day: Jose Villozo. A tough guy, like all those EMT guys, not one to be easily shocked or spooked, but the look in Jose's eyes that night said what he was seeing was shocking, no doubt.

Jose took one look at me and said, voice trembling, "Charlie, Charlie, get in the ambulance! Get in the ambulance."

But not me, not Charlie Morecraft, Mr. Tough Guy. I'm still in freak-out mode, worried about my job, trying to do damage control. So I tell Jose in no uncertain terms, "No, no, Jose, help me! Let's shut off this gauge over here, and help me check out that valve over there…"

And he's looking at me like I'm crazy now. That's when his tone changed to the point where I did a kind of mental "stop, drop, and roll." And with no more trembling now, in a grave voice that made it clear this wasn't a request, Jose said, "No, Charlie, get in that ambulance…"

And still I refused.

Big Girls Don't Cry

Finally, Jose and a few of the other rescue workers forced me face-first onto a gurney and into the back of that ambulance. It just so happened that the EMT driver that night was also a good friend of mine. Her name was Sue. Just like her partner, Jose, Sue was a real professional, a no-nonsense type of Jersey gal, and I remember looking up at Sue for some kind of reassurance. Like maybe it wasn't as bad as Jose and everybody else was saying. That maybe I could just get some aloe vera slathered on my arms and a little Visine to wash out my eyes and still make it to the beach house, you know?

And Sue? Sue was crying, bawling really. And that wasn't like Sue at all. I looked up at her, and I looked back down at myself to see why she might be crying.

Suddenly, I saw my arms. I mean, really saw them for the very first time. And they weren't just black, they were charcoal-broiled black, like steak left too long on the grill. What's more, suddenly they were blistering up and filling with pus and oozing over right in front of my eyes. I could feel my face doing the same thing, blistering and oozing to the point where I could barely see Sue anymore, where I thought the very skin might burst and explode like in some really bad horror movie.

Through a hoarse voice and gurgling throat, I said to Sue, "I guess I'm not so cute anymore, huh, Sue?"

I'm not sure she could understand what I said. It came out as grunts and groans, more like moans, really. They would be the last real words I'd say for a while.

And whether she understood them or not, Sue turned, wailing, and drove through the smoldering flames to rush me to the nearest hospital. Two things happened at that moment: for the very first time I knew I was in serious trouble—and then the pain set in.

The pain? Imagine burning the tip of your finger on a hot burner and the flaring pain, the stinging, that results. Ice cubes can't stop it; nothing can stop it. Now spread that over 45 to 50 percent of your body.

I can't possibly put into words the suffering I endured as the ambulance sped through the night, jostling me to and fro on that gurney, and every inch of my body screaming—howling—in pain as blood and pus and goo stained the starched white sheets beneath me.

There's tough and then there's tough. There's pain and then there's pain. Then there's what I felt. All the way there, I kept screaming to Sue and anyone else who would listen: "Just kill me! Let me die!"

I begged them, pleading, screaming, wailing, but it was no use. It was their job to save people, not kill them. And now, for whatever reason, my survival was their highest priority.

They brought me a quick but endless two miles away to the nearest medical facility, Alexian Brothers Hospital in

Elizabeth, New Jersey. Despite the morphine, the Demerol, and every other painkiller the ER staff pumped into me during those first few frenzied minutes in the emergency room, I still wanted to die, to end the fiery, crackling, burning, stinging, excruciating suffering.

Nothing they gave me even touched the intense, bone-searing pain as they hoisted me from gurney to hospital bed and wheeled me through the silent corridors of that hospital.

Between all the pain and the suffering and the fear that I *did* feel, the one thing I *wasn't* afraid of was death. At that point, I would have welcomed it. I *was* afraid of dying alone, however. I could still speak kind of, sort of, barely. Though my lips were basically burnt off and would require dozens of operations to restore, my lungs hadn't shut down entirely—yet.

I begged every nurse I saw that day to please, please call my wife and kids to let them know what had happened. My hoarse voice was uttering the wish of a dying man. I was certain I was going to die and wanted to at least be in the presence of loved ones when, not if, that was going to happen.

To their credit, the hospital staff moved heaven and earth to track down my family. But through a comedy of errors, everywhere they tried turned out to be a dead end.

First, they tried calling the beach bungalow where my family was staying, but there was no phone there (and this was long before cell phones became popular—or even affordable—for the common man).

Then they tried calling my parents, who lived a town or two away, but it was late at night—hell, early morning now—and they were in bed fast asleep. On a hot August night, with the air-conditioning blasting and the phone all the way in the kitchen, they never heard a thing.

And why would they expect a late-night call anyway? I'd done this a thousand times before, remember? Cool Charlie had always come through with flying colors. Tonight should have been no different; but it was.

My brother and sister were out partying someplace, and so the hospital couldn't get ahold of them, either. And that was that. It was over. I knew right then I was going to die all alone. There would be no happy Hollywood ending for Charlie Morecraft; he'd die bleeding from charred skin in some emergency room, moaning to anyone who would listen to please, someone, put him out of this misery.

Finally, Exxon sent a plant representative to my hometown of Bayonne who wisely went to the police headquarters there. The police were there at my parents' door, waking them up at five in the morning, telling my parents they had to come, that their son was in an accident and they had to come quick. I can only imagine the looks on their faces as they must have garbled out nothing but questions: "Which son? What accident? Where? How?!?"

And my poor mother appalled at having to answer the door in her curlers and housecoat!

The cops also found my brother and sister and corralled them as well; they even tracked down my wife and kids at the Jersey shore. As if it had been scripted in some awful, terrible horror movie, my whole family converged on the hospital at about the same time.

We Are Family

I used to say I got lucky with my parents. I know now that's the wrong term; I was *blessed* by them. I'll never forget hearing my mom the first time she saw me there, lying in the ER ward of the Alexian Brothers Hospital. She rushed into the room, the first to arrive, and took one look at me.

"Thank God," she said, nearly collapsing with relief. "Thank God...that's not my son!"

My own mother didn't recognize me. I never knew that was even possible. As painful as my physical wounds were, the emotional scars ran deep for my mother.

And yet, in the many weeks and months still to come, my mother would be there for all of it—the pain, the sorrow, the rage, the drinking, the not drinking—she would be my rock, an ocean of calm in the middle of my own personal hell.

My dad was no less of a support system in his own fatherly way. My dad was a regular guy, a blue-collar Joe just like me and, I figure, just like most of you reading this today.

My dad was a hustler. He always had two jobs going at the same time, if not three, just so he could give us kids the best of everything growing up. Looking back, we were spoiled brats, but he didn't care. He loved us and wanted the best for us. And we were more than happy to let him give it to us!

He was proud of me, my old man. Especially in school, where I excelled at sports, football in particular. No matter the job, no matter the shift, somehow Dad always managed to sneak away at dinnertime to come see me at practice.

And game nights? Forget about it, nothing could keep Dad away from the sidelines, where he always managed to be pacing, just like the coaches, worrying over every play and celebrating every victory!

On the day of the accident (once Mom realized who I was and called my father in to see me, perhaps for one last time), the first thing Dad said was, "Hang in there, son! I know you. I know how strong you are! I know you can make it."

I'd pretty much given up on living by that point. The fact was, I didn't want to make it. The pain, the agony, the future, it was all too much. But hearing Dad's pep talk, picturing him there on the sidelines as if I was lying there on the playing field in my uniform and not covered in pus and dead skin, I wanted to live.

Suddenly, I wanted my dad to be proud of me one last time. So it was a mystery to me why the rest of my family would continue to support me in the days and weeks following the fire, how Mom would be there by my bed every night, but Dad was MIA.

The doctors told me it was because Dad had a cold and they were concerned about the germs reinfecting me. For a day or two, a week even, I bought it. Even two weeks, okay, but...then I got to thinking: The man had never been sick a day in his life. Had never missed a day of work for as long as I'd known him, and now, suddenly he's skipping out on my recovery?

Something wasn't adding up.

I later learned that right after speaking to me that first night in the hospital, Dad walked out of my room and had a heart attack in the hospital parking lot. That was followed shortly after by a stroke. Dad was never the same.

Really, none of us were.

And not all of us would survive.

Last Rites

Given the severity of the accident, I should have been dead. I mean, I nearly cremated myself, live and in person. Hands, feet, face, hair, neck, ears, you name it, it was burned nearly beyond repair. I spent years trying to figure out how I survived—at first because the pain was so bad I *wanted* to die.

When they brought me to the hospital, I just looked like hell. My face was blown up, parts of me had melted until they were nearly unrecognizable. I was burned over 50 percent of my body. My heart stopped two days in a row, and at one point I almost needed an emergency tracheotomy just to keep breathing.

I was in such bad shape and apparently so close to death

that the nurses wanted me to see the priest for last rites. Even though I was raised a Catholic, I wasn't practicing at the time, so I said, "Hell no. I never needed one before, and I don't need one now. Hit the road."

See, tough guy. But when my mother asked me, begged me to at least let the priest in and hear what he had to say, of course I agreed. ('Cause that's how us tough guys are.)

When the priest came in to see me, I immediately recognized him as the father who was removed from an area parish for allegedly drinking and carousing. *Beautiful*, I thought, *is this poetic justice or what? I'm on my deathbed about to get last rites, and me?*

I get the drunk *priest.*

At this point, I'm lying in the hospital bed, hooked up to every kind of monitor on the planet, just trying to get through the pain. Everything is going downhill, body systems shutting down, teams of doctors trying to figure out which would be the best place for me to die.

I firmly believe I'm about to die, so what is there to lose?

If you can't go out the way you really are, what's the point, right?

The priest began delivering last rites, but I could tell that he was drunk. I mean blotto, so much whiskey on his breath I'm afraid he might light up to smoke and blow me up all over again right there in the hospital, drunk as the guys down at the refinery on payday.

At one point I said to him, trying to lighten the mood a little, "Hey, padre, are you sure this is going to take?"

Because he was drunk at the time, he didn't really see the

joke in that statement and got very angry. Face flushed, eyes struggling to focus, lips covered with spittle, he barked, "Why don't you just die?"

That was it for me.

I.

Went.

Ballistic.

I wanted to kill him, to strangle him. Five seconds earlier I'd been prepared to die; now I was ready to kill someone! I literally, in my condition, tubes and all, machines beeping, IV bags dripping, tried to leap off the gurney to get at this vile man for what he'd just said to me. Priest or no priest, I was out for blood. One minute I was dying, and the next minute I was trying to strangle that guy.

The nurses finally heard all of the commotion and put the priest out of the room, but the damage had already been done. After he left that night, I was a mess.

Is this what people are really thinking, I wondered to myself, *but are just too polite to say to my face?*

Up until that point my wounds had been purely physical, but now they went way beyond skin deep. I hated the priest, I hated God, I hated everyone at that moment. Then a strange thing happened. I stopped wanting to die. Instead of presiding over my demise, that priest had unknowingly given me the motivation to live.

I swore that, no matter what, one day I would get that son of a bitch. And I had to live to keep that promise to myself. So as much as I'd like to say it was divine intervention that saved me that one day, I can't. Instead it was pure anger that helped me make it through those desperate hours right after the accident.

Choosing a Place to Die

After that, things went downhill, fast. I was in a sterile operating theater, splayed out on a hospital bed as the doctors tried anything and everything just to keep me alive.

Alexian Brothers Hospital didn't have a burn unit, so they did the next best thing and put me in an intensive care unit. So there I was in this great, big glassed-in room hooked up to every instrument and monitor they had on the premises, it seemed. IVs, tubes, machines blinking and burping in time, I had it all.

Burn victims eventually go through a swelling process as the body's immune system kicks into gear, fighting to keep it safe by pumping you full of antibodies and other protective fluids. My body swelled all over, but in particular my left arm, which swelled to nearly double its size.

It swelled so badly it was cutting off the circulation in a major artery. Imagine that, all the trauma I'd been through—the chemicals, the explosion, the fire, the pain— and I was going to die from my circulation being cut off? Somebody tell me this is a joke, right?

But it wasn't. To relieve the pressure, the doctors literally took a scalpel and just slit my arm from shoulder to wrist. It was like something out of one of those autopsy specials they show late at night on HBO. Blood sprayed everywhere, and all I could do was lay there in agony and watch it gush like a geyser as the swelling finally went down.

Despite my screams and my begging, there would be no more painkillers for Charlie Morecraft that night. I had been given too many already, and they wouldn't give me any more. I couldn't be given anesthesia, either, because the doctors thought I wouldn't wake up. I had to watch and endure every lifesaving procedure as if I hadn't taken a single painkiller at all.

It was like those battlefield scenes you'll see in old Civil War movies where the field doctor has to amputate some poor soldier's leg without any painkillers. Hey, at least those guys got to bite down on a bullet; I didn't even get that common courtesy!

What I did get, all joking aside, was one of the best medical teams available on the planet, bar none. Suddenly doctors converged from everywhere to save my life and to prepare for what little future I might have left after they got through with me. Not only were there doctors from Alexian Brothers at my bedside that night, but also from Exxon's crack medical staff and, of course, the nearby Saint Barnabas burn unit.

Of course, before this expert team of expert surgeons and burn specialists could treat me, they first had to decide where I was going to die. I kid you not: there was an argument between this all-star team of doctors as to where I would be better off.

Some doctors argued that if I stayed put, I would die at Alexian Brothers. Others argued that if they tried to transport me to the burn unit at Saint Barnabas, I would die on the way. And they stood there arguing about where I would die.

Die here or die there!

At some point the doctors could see they were upsetting me so they took this "discussion" into the hall. Great timing, guys. It was at that very moment that I chose to make good on their argument; I was dying as they argued about where I should die.

Literally, I could feel my body slowly shutting down. One by one, my limbs stopped feeling so painful. While I was grateful for any relief from the pain, I knew that no pain meant no circulation, and that wasn't good. It was as if the blood had stopped flowing to one arm, then the next; one leg, then the next.

Unfortunately, it stopped inside my chest as well. Then my lungs shut down. I could feel myself dying inch by inch, and the best doctors in a hundred-mile radius were one wall away from doing me any good.

I didn't care. Let them argue, let my vital systems shut down. Just let me die. I knew what was facing me if I was "lucky" enough to survive: the long months of recovery, the surgeries, the skin grafts, the pain and suffering, and disfiguration. Frankly, at that point, I didn't want any part of it.

If this was my destiny, then death was doing me a favor. Eventually one of the doctors looked in and saw my condition. They rushed in, unified once more, and did everything they could to save my life—a needle full of Adrenalin in the chest, drugs up the wazoo, the whole ball of wax.

It worked, and they made the decision then and there to transfer me to the Saint Barnabas burn unit before my condition could deteriorate even further. (There was a *further*?!) They did so as soon as they could that morning, and the next phase of my recovery began.

The Burn Unit

The burn unit at Saint Barnabas is located underground, where the special bariatric pressure chambers known as "debriding tanks" are located. Once you arrive on-site, they literally wheel you back down this long alley like a meat wagon making a special delivery and then unload you.

A crane picks you and the stretcher up at the same time and hoists you into what's known, for very good reason, as the tanking room. That's because it's full of these great, big hover tanks, four of them in all. Inside each tank are water, Clorox, and different antibiotics.

The crane slowly, carefully lowers you into this tank, and the pain starts immediately.

The tanking room was full when I entered Saint Barnabas: twelve people just like you and I who said accidents happen to other people, who said it would never happen to them. By the time I left treatment there to enter rehab four floors upstairs, nine of the people who were there that night had died. Three of us walked out of that room to live our lives; the other nine never got the privilege.

To this day, I'm still not sure if we were the lucky ones.

I don't care what time of year you're reading this, day or night, spring or fall, if you were to call Saint Barnabas today, right now, you'd find all those tanks full. What's worse, there's a waiting list to get in one of them!

There were four debriding tanks in the room, and twelve people waiting to use them. It was like Russian roulette. We never knew when we'd go in, but could only judge by our place in line as to how long it might be before the torture began.

We lay there, stretched out on gurneys, listening to the screams of the four people already in the tanks. They were inhuman screams, and once I got in the fourth tank, I would find out why.

Later, that hallway outside the tanking room would become a nightmare within a nightmare. If what happened inside the tanks was bad, then waiting to go into one of them was, if anything, worse. Not only did you know the pain you were going to experience, but also you were trying to time your morphine shot so that it would kick in right as they were lowering you into the water.

Sometimes you'd guess it right, and the pain wouldn't be quite so excruciating. Other times you'd get it wrong, and it wouldn't have kicked in by the time they started scrubbing your skin off layer by layer. Or the painkiller would have worn off by the time they dunked you in, and you knew you were going to feel every rip, tear, shred, and searing ounce of pain from the curing but hellish waters full of bleach and antibiotics.

I was in the Burn Center at Saint Barnabas for three

months after the fire. I had survived hell on earth after nearly cremating myself on the job, but I had no idea what I was in for on my first day at the Burn Center.

The fact is, most burn victims don't die from the fire itself, they die from infections in their severe wounds *after* the fire. Your skin isn't just good for suntans and tattoos, it's also your body's best line of defense against germs and infections.

When it's damaged or, in the case of a burn victim, exposed, open, and raw, there is no line of defense; every germ is potentially lethal. In order to keep my skin fresh and infection-free, the wounds—the open, exposed, raw wounds—had to be cleaned every day.

Well, *cleaned* sounds so safe and sound, so harmless and sterile, so painless. More accurately, I had to endure the torturous process known as "debriding," or cutting away the dead skin.

Yes, I said it: "cutting away."

The dead skin.

Every day.

Although they looked harmless enough, the four stainless steel tanks in the tanking room were full of water, bleach, and antibiotics, a healing cocktail that was deadly painful to those with open wounds. And from the waist up, my entire body was one big open wound.

There are no words to describe the pain I experienced in those tanks every single day. Words like *tearing* and *slashing* and *ripping* and *scraping* barely do the pain justice; words like *searing* and *agonizing* and *excruciating* and *unbearable* only hint at the severity of what I was feeling as the burn nurses sliced, peeled, and tore away at the scar tissue that covered my burns.

At Exxon, I'd never worn my protective gear because I thought it made me look wimpy and I preferred to look tough, hard, macho. In the tank, there was no such thing.

There was no shame in screaming; it was a natural response to such intense physical pain. I can't imagine working there and hearing those screams, those harsh, guttural, animal screams bouncing off the tank walls day in and day out.

As each layer of dead skin was scraped off in the tank, the water would wash over the open wound intensifying the pain the way opening a baking oven turns a sunburn from uncomfortable to unbearable.

And while the physical pain was excruciating, while I never thought there could be anything worse, I knew there was something worse after that first day: climbing into the tank the next day. And the day after that.

I think we can all endure intense pain once. It's easier, if not exactly easy, to endure something like that if you know there's a light at the end of the tunnel, if someone says to you, "Okay, just one more layer of skin and we're done." But there was no light at the end of the tunnel, there was no "done," only, "Okay, just one more layer of skin and we're done...for today."

I screamed in that tank the first day, and I cried myself to sleep in bed that night. I'm not ashamed to say it; you would, too. Not because of the pain, although that was beyond agonizing, but because I knew I would have to endure the same pain the next day.

After a while I didn't know which was worse: the dread of being in the tank or being in the tank itself; lying on a gurney in the hallway, listening to the screams of those poor souls already in the tank; or being lowered into the tank itself. It was an endless cycle with no relief in sight. No matter how much salve was rubbed on the open wounds, they still hurt. No matter how many painkillers they gave me, they never touched the pain. Not really. And nothing, I mean nothing, could erase the memory of what had happened in the tank the day before as you crawled into it the next morning.

In my saner moments, during those rare times when I could think clearly, I would pray, "Dear Lord, I hope no one I care for ever has to go through this."

The only thing more painful was knowing it could have all been avoided if only I'd been less of a tough guy and paid more attention to safety on the job.

"It'll Never Happen to Them, Either."

My roommate at Saint Barnabas was a man named Louis. Louis was in a motorcycle accident. He blew a stop sign on the way to somewhere very important—we always think where we're going is so damn important, don't we?—and ran into a car. When he did, the gas tank on the motorcycle exploded. So did Louis.

That's how Louis "went up." That's what we called it in the burn unit: "going up." "How'd you go up?," "I went up like this…," "I went up like that…" It was shorthand, I suppose, so we didn't have to use words like *fire* or *burn* or *scar*.

Jim was there at the same time as me and Louis. [I've changed many of the names in this book to protect the privacy of those who do not wish to be as public about their pain as myself.] Jim was just another regular guy, wanting to have a summer BBQ. He started his gas grill, realized he'd forgotten his matches, ran back inside to get them, and left his grill on while he was gone.

Why not, right? Too much trouble turning it off again, then turning it back on. I mean, what would it have taken Jim to do it the right way, the safe way? Another whole thirty seconds both times? When he came back and struck a match, he went up—courtesy of all that gas that had built up while he was gone getting the matches.

Courtney was another girl who was there with me in the burn unit at the same time. She was young, only eighteen or nineteen. How did she go up? Courtney was pledging a sorority and eager to attend a costume ball. Her sisters dressed her up like a mummy, covering her in gauze and rags from head to toe.

While she was at the party, having a good time, looking forward to a long life of such social interaction, Courtney backed into a match while a fellow partygoer was lighting a cigarette; that's how she went up.

She was burned over 90 percent of her body.

Unfortunately, Courtney lived. Or I guess I should say, Courtney "survived." There's not much living in what Courtney's doing; then or now.

Don't get me wrong. Life is a precious gift. None of us should take it for granted, and under normal circumstances, nobody should ever wish it away. But fire is not a normal circumstance, and I believe in my heart of hearts that that poor girl would have been better off dead.

And if you think I'm armchair quarterbacking, know this: I still keep in touch with that young woman today, and I truly, honestly, sincerely believe that Courtney would agree with me.

It's a bitter pill to swallow, but sometimes dying is better.

For proof, you need only to ask the living.

I often felt the same about my own fate. Would I have been better off dead? Ask me now, I'll say, "Hell no! I'm glad I survived!" Ask me back then, and you would have gotten a very different answer. Every day, every night, all day, all night, I wanted to die. Period. I obsessed about it.

They say every so often death takes a holiday. Not at Saint Barnabas. There are no days off in the burn unit, not one. Every day—birthday, anniversary, Halloween, Christmas, Fourth of July—you have to go into the tank for debriding.

I was there at Saint Barnabas for three months.

You know who else was there for three months? My mother. Every night I'd come up from one of the tanks and Mom would be there, wringing her hands, purse on her lap, waiting patiently for me.

I couldn't have been much company. When I wasn't crying, I was complaining, when I wasn't complaining, I was shivering uncontrollably or tossing and turning or cursing my fate, God, and the world.

It didn't matter what I said or how I cursed or screamed or howled, Mom was there. Other family members came and went, most of them never to return. Who could blame them? I wasn't much to look at and even worse to be around. But Mom? Every night, I could count on her to be there. That woman saved my life as sure as I'm writing these words today.

After three months, I was moved up to the fourth floor of the hospital, or what's known as a "step-down" floor. That's where they try to bring you back to a normal hospital life. Not a normal life, but a normal hospital life, which means you're now out of hot water enough that they can begin to rehabilitate you.

Lucky me.

Down in the burn unit, it's merely lifesaving measures. There's no TLC or rehab down there. The reason the old skin is ripped off is to save the new skin from getting infected. It's all about infection because infection means death.

You know those nine poor souls who didn't survive? That's what the good folks down in the burn unit are trying to prevent; really, that's *all* they're trying to prevent. Up on the fourth floor, it was still survival but also more about recovery. You're out of the woods; now it's time to get you ready to go back into the world—someday.

The explosion was so intense that I had been burned to the bone, so I had a lot of orthopedic bone surgeries done while there on the fourth floor. Skin grafts as well. Not the cosmetic kind to make you look presentable—that came much, much later—but just to get new skin on fresh bone.

There was also extensive, daily, and painful physical therapy. Jesus, just saying the words *physical therapy* turns my stomach, even all these years later. When you burn, when your body experiences that kind of searing, destroying, intense heat, the muscles literally clench up.

When firefighters find dead bodies in burned houses, they are nearly always in the fetal position. Not because the victims are trying to shield or protect themselves from the intense heat, but because the fire dehydrates the body's muscles, causing them to contract and literally clench up. Firefighters, EMTs, and even coroners often call this the "boxer's posture."

I had it, too, so much of my time on the fourth floor was spent in physical therapy with therapists literally forcing my arms and legs down to prevent the boxer's posture from reoccurring.

Moving stiff muscle that, by the way, does *not* want to be moved is like breaking and resetting a bone, only on purpose and daily. It was like the tanks all over, excruciating pain over and over, day in, day out.

Eventually I was shipped to nearby Kessler Institute for Rehabilitation to recover and move forward from the rehab I'd endured at Saint Barnabas. Of all the hospitals I've been to, before and since, Kessler was then and is still now the worst. Not because of the doctors, the nurses, or even the facility itself, but because of the sad stories of the other patients there.

My roommate at the time was a young guy, barely nineteen. His name was Willy. Willy had left a party drunk to hop on his motorcycle and head back home; he never made it. Instead, he dumped the bike about a mile down the road, hit the asphalt, and became an instant paraplegic.

Willy was in Kessler trying to learn to get around by steering a wheelchair with his chin, because he couldn't move his body—any of it—from the neck down.

Every day I thought I had it bad, every time I wanted to feel sorry for myself, all I had to do was look one bed over and count my lucky stars. But this kid? Willy had nowhere to look but in the mirror. He couldn't even run away from himself, couldn't even throw himself out a window to get away from the endless thoughts that must have racked his young brain.

Another patient at Kessler was a guy just like me, just like you probably, too, who thought accidents would never happen to him, least of all not in his own home. A hobbyist, Phil built model boats and planes in his basement. He even had a little grinding wheel set up down there.

He wore no glasses or gloves, and why would he? After all, he had used that grinder for years. But there was a flaw in the grinding wheel, and one day when he least expected it, grinding away on another new project he would proudly add to his growing mantelpiece upstairs, the wheel blew apart and hit his face, mainly his eyes.

He was blinded as a result of that accident.

He was at Kessler trying to get around with one of those long white canes with the red tip. And me? I was there. I had survived, and it left me plenty of time to wonder how and why I'd gotten there in the first place.

Scars? Souvenirs? What's the Difference?

People ask me why I hated Kessler rehab so much. Again, it wasn't the people who worked there or even the pain I endured as my new surgeries healed or my limbs grew more flexible. No, it was the patients who suffered there. Every night after a long day of rehab, my roommate Willy would lie in bed, unable to move, crying himself to sleep.

I'm a father myself so my first instinct was to say something to reassure him, to make him feel better, to lighten his load. Not that I was in any great mental shape at the time, believe me. I hated the world with a passion, blamed everyone and everything else but myself for the fire, for my current situation, but the least I could have done was lend a helping hand. After all, I could still move mine.

I never said a word; I never did a thing. In all that time, I never offered him those fatherly words of advice I rehearsed in my head each night as I quietly fell asleep to the sound of Willy's tears. I was paralyzed as well, petrified by the fear of saying the wrong thing or something not quite right enough.

And so I stayed silent and tough night after night.

But what do you say to a kid in the prime of his life who will never move his fingers or his toes, let alone know the touch of a woman or get a hug from his kids?

What do you say to a man who's blind and will never see his children again? Or any of those model ships and planes he built before his grinding wheel blew up in his face?

In a way, it was a lot like how I'd always felt on the line back at Exxon. How a lot of us felt, a lot of us working guys who thought we were "too tough" to reach out to the next guy and tell him, "Hey, Joe, put on your safety glasses."

Or, "Hey, Grady, where's your harness?"

Or, "Hey, Charlie, roll down your damn sleeves!"

Guys who did that, we thought they were wimps. Or worse, they were usually management. And no one who earned a paycheck for a living wanted to sound like *them*. So we'd keep our mouths shut, and let the guy work without gloves or a hard hat or whatever the hell else he was supposed to be wearing.

It was kind of like a code of silence—do nothing, say nothing, look macho, stay cool—and no one spoke it better than me; than Cool Charlie. I guess, up there in my room at Kessler, I was still speaking it. (Or not speaking, as the case may be.)

Trust me, I couldn't wait to leave that rehab unit.

I went back to Saint Barnabas for the bulk of my reconstructive surgery, and there was a ton of it. Forty, forty-five, then some fifty surgeries later, I can see out of my left eye again, and I can hear out of my left ear again. To look at me now is to see a picture of normalcy; to look at me then was a horror show.

My nose, my lips, most of my face has been rebuilt to look normal. Looking at pictures of myself before the accident, I hardly recognize my old self. I've been looking at my new self for so long now.

My mouth in particular has been reworked from the ground up. That night, running through the flames that covered me, I tried to hold my breath, realizing I'd ruin my lungs if I let the fire inside.

After a minute or two I gave in and gulped the hot, fiery air inside, not only damaging my lungs, but also searing my lips, my tongue, my gums. All had to be significantly repaired to look and feel normal. Even to sound normal. My voice, my pronunciation, my delivery, all evolved along with my lips and the evolving shape of my mouth.

To think, this guy who could only gargle and groan for months in the hospital now earns his living flying all over the country speaking about safety. It's nothing short of amazing, and it's still going on. My face, my limbs, my skin, it's still evolving. Last year I had no less than six surgeries as a direct result of my injuries. Can you imagine? Thirty years later now, and I'm still in rehab?

Recently I got a new chin for Christmas; not long after getting the contract for this book, I had another surgical procedure done on my thigh. I'll have more surgeries, perhaps a half-dozen or so, by the time this book comes out. And I still won't be done.

'Til Death Do Us Part

Finally, dozens of surgeries later, the doctors at Saint Barnabas were going to let me out to attend my brother's wedding. Wedding? Jesus, I'd missed everything else—the engagement, the parties, the celebrations, the family events—all because I'd been in rehab or the tanks or trying to get my life back together. Meanwhile, it seemed, everyone else's was right on track.

I was excited; it would be my first "field trip" in nearly a year of extensive recovery and rehab. For the first time in that year, I'd get to stand there, shoulder to shoulder with my brother Jerry and hug him, man to man. Here I thought I was dead and now this?

But there was a catch. To prevent infection and reduce scarring on my sensitive "new" skin, I would have to wear what's called a Jobst suit from head to toe, including a full facial mask, for an entire year.

This mask isn't sexy, either, like that slick *Phantom of the Opera* mask or some hotshot superhero's; it's dull and tight and supposed to be flesh colored, but really isn't. It's the color of panty hose and about as sexy but two or three times as thick. And it's skintight.

It's elastic and blunt and ugly and all kinds of uncomfortable and seriously awkward. Here I was, a guy who'd roll up his flame-retardant sleeves because they were too uncomfortable, and now I'm covered head to toe in a suit that puts the *hell* back in *hellish*. Anyone who thinks God doesn't have a sense of humor, I'm here to make you think again.

I hated that mask, hated it, but I couldn't take it off. What I hated the most, I suppose, was that it meant my recovery still wasn't over, that I still wasn't in the clear.

And I was ready to be in the clear. I had a life now. I'd committed to living after those long, dark days in the hospital, then in rehab. I had a wife, two beautiful daughters. I had to learn how to provide for them, somehow go back to work or find something to do.

I had friends who wanted to see me, guys from work. I had my brother's wedding to attend, places to go, people to see...and all in a rubbery, fleshy, clingy ski mask?

I'd walk around like Frankenstein, folks staring and gawking at me. It got so bad I had to bring a preprinted card with me medically authorizing that I was to wear this suit and this mask.

Think about it: there are certain places where it's not quite safe to walk in wearing a flesh-colored ski mask, if you know what I mean. Banks, for one. Imagine me going into First Savings, the bank in the town where I grew up, and showing the security guard this card.

And he'd open the door for me—that is, if he didn't shoot me first!—and escort me to the teller to do my banking. I hated it because I was a spectacle for folks to gawk at, stare at, and discuss.

It was like that everywhere I went: the grocery store, the movies, the bank, the gas station. Didn't matter, folks would gawk and stare, kids would point and be curious. I was like the Elephant Man of Jersey!

But getting the suit off after that long, degrading year

didn't help much. I might have felt more comfortable out of the suit, but I still had to find a way to fit into the skin I was in.

Back at Exxon, grateful to have a job to go to every day, I'd be changing in the locker room, getting into my work clothes, and notice the guys staring at my scars.

I know they didn't mean anything by it because, seriously...how could they not stare? But still, I was self-conscious, and unlike the Jobst suit, I couldn't merely take these scars off after a year.

They were mine for life.

CHAPTER 4

Smoldering Embers— a Family in Denial

But I *had* a life at least, and for that I was grateful. What they don't tell you in rehab, in the tank or the step-down floor, is what to do when you get home. They can fix your body, but they can't get in your head. And frankly, that's where I needed the most help of all.

How to act around your family, what they'll be going through, what they've already been through, how to explain to your kids why Daddy looks like this, how to explain to your wife that it hurts too much to express your physical love for her.

There's no pamphlet or brochure called *Life on the Outside*, but I sure needed one! Because outside those hospital walls, there was a whole life waiting on me. One that had been put on hold for the long, endless months I'd been in rehab.

All the problems I'd had before the accident were still there on pause, waiting for my return. What's more, my family had been dealing with them on their own. And they hadn't been under the influence the whole time like I had, either.

They'd been dealing with it all, day by day, without their old man around. Sometimes I wonder if that wasn't a blessing, given what their husband and father was really like.

And in many ways, my family's scars ran far deeper than mine and for a pretty good reason. Because Cool Charlie? He came with a lot of baggage, and it didn't just start with the fire. No, it started a long time before that, and they'd been there for most of it.

The fact was, Charlie Morecraft wasn't just cool. For most of his life, for far too long, in fact, he'd also been an alcoholic.

A Buried Secret; an Uncertain Future

I was never drunk on the job, and I certainly wasn't drunk on the night of my accident. I was what's known as a functioning alcoholic. I could maintain, I could cope, I could say when and where I'd stop or start drinking, but that didn't make me any less of a threat.

You see, when alcoholics lie, deny, and alibi—or what I like to call the alcoholic's "creed"—they don't just do it about drinking, they do it about everything else in their life as well. It gets easy after a while to lie, deny, and alibi about everything else as well.

"I didn't do it."

"It wasn't my fault."

"That's not my responsibility."

"I don't handle that department."

"I was somewhere else."

"It was so-and-so's fault."

These are the words I was tempted to say often and believably on or off the job. My words were believable because I was often sober when I said them, I meant them sincerely, and after all, I was Cool Charlie.

Who wouldn't believe me?

"Eat, Drink, and Be Merry..."

My favorite saying once upon a time used to be an oldie but a goodie: "Eat, drink, and be merry because tomorrow you may die." It was more than a saying; it was a lifestyle.

And although I was never, ever drunk on the job, my drunken attitude followed me everywhere. The same lies, denials, and alibis I told about drinking carried over into work. The same excuses I made for myself were used to justify my attitude on site.

I may not have been drunk, but I was certainly just as selfish in my attitudes and wants and desires on site as I was at any liquor store, sports pub, or dive bar.

And every drunk, sober or inebriated, thinks the same thing: nothing will happen to me. I'll never get stopped by the cops. I can hit the brakes in time to avoid hitting that mailbox or parked car or the kid who just ran into the road. I'm in control, I'm in power...I'm okay.

The worst drunken behavior to follow me onto the job was that inevitable and unjustified sense of invincibility. Nothing will ever happen to me.

Alcohol didn't make me bypass procedures that night. Alcohol didn't make me take shortcuts. Alcohol didn't make me ignore my safety equipment. But being an alcoholic did.

So many people think the drink is the problem. It's not. It's the drinker. It's his or her individual makeup, internal chemistry, emotional baggage, family dynamics, and even genetics that account for who is and who isn't more susceptible to becoming an alcoholic.

We all know folks who can sit at a bar, have their two-drink maximum, and never reach for that third. Likewise, we all know those folks who can't stop at two; who can't stop at two dozen; who can't stop until they've emptied their pockets, alienated all their friends, abused the bartender, and closed the place down.

I never set out to become an alcoholic. All I ever wanted to do was to go out with family or friends and drink just enough until I got to that point where everything and everybody, especially me, was just a little bit cooler.

You know that point you get to: Everything is just a little better. You're better. You feel smarter, better looking, and cooler than you did when you first sat down at the bar. People like you more, women like you more, you can tell a joke and have the whole bar laughing, everything is happening in your direction, you're on fire and on point and in the fun zone.

That's the goal I was always shooting for. Problem is, that fun zone is a moving target. Some nights it only takes a few cocktails to get there; other nights, every bottle behind the bar and you still miss it.

You know that show *Cheers*, where everybody knows your name and they're all just buzzed enough, but never too drunk or sloppy or messy or incoherent? That's what I was looking for, a kind of alcohol nirvana, but like any mirage, I could never find it.

That didn't stop me from looking!

Birth of a Drinker

I didn't start drinking until college. And I can still remember quite clearly the first time I drank socially. There was a big dance that night, and I was petrified. For one, I couldn't dance, didn't know how and knew I'd never learn. What's more, I was scared of women.

Not on a one-on-one sense per se—I'd dated in high school and knew my way around dinner and a movie—but en masse in a dance situation? At college? It felt like the big leagues, and I'd just been called up from the minors.

Luckily one of the guys went out and bought a bottle of rye. We mixed it with some 7UP and finished the bottle before we headed up to the dance. On the way into the auditorium, I saw a gorgeous girl standing just inside the doorway.

I walked right up to her—it helps to have a few shots of courage in you—and said something I'd never said before: "Hey, beautiful, wanna dance?"

Now, an hour earlier I could barely speak, but suddenly I was the bravest man in the world. I'd never been so cocky or full of swagger with a girl before in my life, but it worked. She said, "Yes!"

And I was on my way. I often wonder what my future might have been like if that ballsy move hadn't worked, if I'd gotten shot down as a mouthy drunk or had one too many shots that night and passed out before the dance.

Would my lucky streak have ended right there? Would my later descent into alcoholism have been avoided because I'd crashed and burned my very first time out of the bottle?

I guess we'll never know. Because for now I'd stumbled onto the secret formula to success. All I had to do was drink just enough to get me to that point, that place of self-confidence, where I could talk to anyone and be endearing, say anything and be charming, and do those things I'd never have the courage to do without a drink in my hand.

For a while, it was easy to find that spot. A couple belts before a dance or a social, a couple more during a date that was going really, really well. But like everything else in life, once your body gets used to a certain amount of something, it always wants more.

If you're a coffee drinker, you always need just one more cup. If you're a smoker, you can't stick to half a pack of cigarettes without always wanting just one more. If you've got a sweet tooth, there comes a point where one piece of chocolate or candy just doesn't cut it.

So it is with alcohol as well. Pretty soon, to get to that cool spot I loved so much, I needed an extra shot of courage just to get out the door in the afternoon, and one last nightcap before I went to bed. If one drink was good, then two was better, and three was great, and four was sublime, and on and on it went.

One for the Road

Life was good for a while. I attended college, met a great gal, got a job with a great company called Exxon, and settled down. Gone were the crazy college days of partying until dawn, but I still managed to find that cool spot for myself, even if I eventually crossed the line from time to time.

Even after my two daughters were born, I could still keep it in line, for the most part. Sure, Daddy had a little too much during those backyard barbecues or while putting together the toys on Christmas Eve, but...who didn't?

I wasn't an alcoholic; I couldn't be. After all, I was an adult now. I had a house, a mortgage, a loving wife, two beautiful daughters, a great job, two cars. I was living the dream.

I was a success story, so how could I have a drinking problem?

I should have had all the natural confidence in the world, but old habits die hard. I still needed those three or four—or five or six or even seven—shots of courage to get to my happy place.

Eventually, however, that cool feeling—and sobriety in general—got harder and harder to maintain. I got sloppy and unpleasant and, frankly, out of control.

There was just enough Cool Charlie left inside when I got ugly to ignore Wasted Charlie, and I had enough sense to apologize and make promises—to lie, deny, and alibi— to keep my family happy.

So what if I ruined a few birthday parties or dinged up the family car weaving home from the corner bar or skipped a few of the girls' soccer games with a "headache"? I was still a good husband, a great father, and an excellent provider, right?

It's amazing how lucky I was in those golden, hazy years. I cringe now to think of all the near misses, of all the boozy drives, and the friends who kept me out of this fight or took the heat for me when I blew off a family dinner to close down O'Grady's or O'Houlihan's or O'Dooley's one last time.

But every hot streak has to end sometime, right?

Eventually, the problem got too big, too obnoxious, for folks to ignore any longer. People started to notice. My family started to have secret code words among themselves for Daddy's drinking. There were blackouts and incidents and a general tone of ugliness every time that ice started to clink in Daddy's favorite glass. That should have been it for me; I should have thrown in the towel right there.

Lots of people do; they give up when booze starts bringing them down. They say, "This isn't for me; it's not my bag. I can't handle my liquor, and I've hurt too many people too many times. It was fun while it lasted, but hey, I'll just stick to coffee and tea from now on." Not Charlie Morecraft. I did what any other respectable family man who's been borrowing courage from the bottle for half his life would do. I sat down, assessed the situation, adapted, and eventually...overcame.

I told myself, "Look, if the hard stuff is getting to you, lay off it. Stick to beer instead." It was a real lightbulb moment—problem solved! And it worked, at least for a little while.

But when you're an alcoholic, switching drinks is a little like speeding down a mountain in a sports car with no brakes. Switching gears isn't really going to help. Eventually you're still going to crash once you get to the bottom. The only variable is how long it takes to get there.

Unfortunately, I was a long way from bottom. It didn't make the ride down the mountain any less harrowing or, for my family and friends, less ugly.

"Maybe I Have a Problem..."

When beer still got me in trouble, I switched to light beer. When light beer wasn't the magic bullet, I tried wine. White wine, red wine, Zinfandel, or Chianti, it didn't really matter. Things still got ugly. It wasn't the drink that was the problem, it was the drinker.

There's a saying about relationships that has always stuck with me ever since the first time I heard it: "Wherever you go, there you are." In other words, whether you're hopping from bed to bed or bar to bar, from beer to wine or whiskey, you're still the same guy with the same problems, fears, doubts, and insecurities looking into the bottom of that empty glass.

We always think a new partner or a new job or winning the lottery or that one, last drink is going to get us there to the ultimate cool place, where it's no longer temporary but permanent. But that's like trying to catch one of those shimmering pools of heat on a hot, dusty desert road—the closer you get, the faster you drive, it's always a foot or two just out of reach.

And so it was with my drinking. Every Monday I'd trudge off to work, hungover and promising never to disappoint my family, my girls, ever again. And I'd be good for a day or two.

Then a couple of guys from the refinery would be heading over to Chauncy's or Maguire's or Finnegan's or McSherry's on the way home from work, and by Wednesday, I was right back in it. Making excuses, blaming and denying, lying and alibiing.

One shift drink would lead to two, would lead to three. Dinner would come and go, and before I knew it, my coworkers were gone and I was closing the place down with a sullen group of random strangers.

Another family night ruined. Another round of explaining to do when I got home or called my wife for a ride and had to leave my car overnight in the bar's parking lot again.

And after one hangover too many, I stopped and thought to myself, *Maybe I do have a problem, after all.* I didn't do anything about it, but at least the seeds had been planted.

Not too long after that, I saw one of those "You may be an alcoholic if…" questionnaires in a magazine. With trembling hands I read it greedily. And the very first sign that you may be an alcoholic was "Do you experience blackouts?"

Psssht, no! I wasn't some Bowery bum passed out in the gutter with no idea how he got there. Of course, many was the time after a football game at Giants Stadium when I had to wait for everyone to leave the parking lot so I could actually find my car, but everybody forgets where they park from time to time, right?

So, phew, I was no alcoholic.

Then I read the second sign: "Do you ever drink alone after hiding your drinking from others?" That got a big, fat no as well. After all, from that first college dance onward, my whole reason for drinking period was to socialize, to feel confident around others, to mix and mingle with absolute freedom. If I did drink alone, it was to get geared up for whatever social event was on that night's agenda, and I avoided doing that as often as possible.

Third sign: "Are you irresponsible at work? And/or have you ever lost a job because of alcohol?" This question was almost offensive. I mean, at the time I was reading that magazine article, I'd never been more valuable at work.

I had job security up the wazoo because I was literally the go-to guy for the dangerous, the dirty, the hazardous, the must-get-done-today gigs. Well, me and Pete that is.

If you wanted something dirty done, fast and cheap, Pete and I were your men. The dynamic duo was at your service, and don't think we weren't in high demand because of our reputation as fixers, not whiners.

So was I suffering at work because of alcohol? Hell no. Not only had booze introduced me to my good buddy Pete, but it had bonded us into one of the best and most valuable teams at the plant. No, I wasn't an alcoholic, no way.

"Do you drink in the morning?" According to the magazine questionnaire, this was the fourth sign that you just might be an alcoholic. Now, for this one I needed a little "rational leeway."

Have you ever heard that Alan Jackson song? You know, the one he sings with Jimmy Buffett called "It's Five O'Clock Somewhere"? That was kind of my answer. See, back then I was a shift worker. Day shift, night shift, double time, overtime, weekends, and holidays, I worked them all.

Oftentimes my shift ended just as everyone else's day was beginning. Frequently it was still dark out. So, to my way of thinking, it was still nighttime. So if I stopped off at the convenience store and grabbed a six-pack before heading home, that wasn't morning drinking, that was after-work drinking.

And if I got off a night shift late and didn't start drinking until one or two in the morning, well...it was still dark out, so again, call me a night drinker, an early drinker, a late drinker, a shift drinker, but never a morning drinker.

No, it was clear—four questions, not a definitive "yes" answer in the bunch. I was no alcoholic. At least, not as long as I was able to lie, deny, and alibi. Sure, I might have forgotten where I'd parked at Giants Stadium a time or two, to say nothing of how I got there. And maybe I drink alone in order to go drink some more with others, and maybe technically it was morning when I had my first drink of the day, but it was always after work, right?

I often wondered how others might have answered that questionnaire for me. What my wife would have said in response to those four questions? Or my two beautiful daughters? My boss? My neighbors? My favorite bartenders? How would Pete, my partner in crime and half of the dynamic duo, have answered?

But of course, I never asked. Better to fool myself and not invite others to be a part of the lie. Then again, before too long, it wouldn't be just some random magazine quiz forcing me to face reality; it would be the cops.

"Do You Know Who I Am?"

It had finally happened. I'd landed in jail. There I was, courtesy of the state of New Jersey, standing in the drunk tank, literally rattling a tin cup against the bars of my cell to get the guard's attention.

Here I was, the nonalcoholic, in jail on a drunk-driving ticket.

Over the sounds of my tin cup clanging against the bars of my cell, I screamed out to anyone who would listen, "Do you know who I am?"

The guard looked back at me and without pausing said, "Yeah, I know who you are. You're a drunk in a jail cell."

For the first time, I couldn't lie to myself. This was no cheap magazine feature or do-it-yourself questionnaire; this was the cold, hard truth. I sat in that cell and tried to shrink into the corner so nobody would notice me.

I was embarrassed. This guard was right. I was just another drunk in a cell. How many did he see in an average night? In a typical week? A dozen? Two dozen? Fifty? A hundred?

How many of those drunks asked this same guy, "Do you know who I am?" How many of them sat back down, tin cup in hand, to stare at their empty future on the bottom of last night's shoes?

More than being embarrassed, I was furious with myself. Drinking and driving? Thank God I'd only wound up in the drunk tank with a ticket and not some poor innocent kid in the morgue. Who might I have hurt or endangered while drinking and driving?

And how many times had it happened before?

No Problem?

After I got out of that jail cell, I decided enough was enough. If this was my rock bottom, better it wound up being just a ticket—and a wake-up call—and not a life sentence for vehicular manslaughter. I was so embarrassed and ashamed, so furious with myself. I knew I had to take a stand.

I'd had it with drinking. I could no longer deny that I had a problem, so I decided to quit, no problem. I'd done it before. I had tons of willpower when I wanted to and wasn't a stranger to going cold turkey when things got out of hand.

When I'd decided to quit smoking a few years back, there was no nicotine gum or patch to help me. I just quit cold turkey, no problem. If my pants started getting tight and I felt like losing a little weight, I just stopped eating, no problem.

So I just quit drinking, just like that. No problem. I even had a goal. Somewhere along the line, I remembered reading that if you could go ninety days without drinking, you probably didn't have a problem.

Okay, I worked better with a goal in mind. So ninety days it was. And ninety days I did. It was as simple as crossing each day off on a calendar, which I literally did. Three months went by like that—ninety marks on the calendar pages over my desk.

I'd done it, no problem. And on the ninety-first day I went out and celebrated. Guess how? Sure, I had a drink. A couple of drinks, which turned into a big party, and well, I don't need to tell you the rest.

The point was, I'd proven to myself that the cop was wrong; I wasn't a drunk. Because everyone knows that drunks can't stop drinking—not for ninety days, not for nine days, not for one day. I could stop. I'd done it, and now I knew the secret behind the secret: control.

If I could just control my drinking, I could avoid being a drunk. I could avoid drunk-driving tickets and jail cells and the shame and scorn and judgment of my family and friends. I guess I forgot the old adage: "When you have to control something, it's out of control."

The more control I applied, it seemed, the worse my drinking got. At some point in this blur of stopping and starting drinking, of binging and more binging, I started to spiral out of control.

The only way I was able to keep any semblance of control during this period was through the help, support, and frankly, enabling of my family, my friends, even my co-workers. Don't get me wrong; I'm not blaming them.

God bless them, they just loved me and wanted to save my ass, even if I could have cared less what happened to myself at that point in my life. But like so many well-meaning loved ones who enable an alcoholic, their commitment to keeping me in control allowed me to spiral out of control at an almost blinding rate.

Where once upon a time, it was my job to lie, deny, and alibi, now it became theirs. While I was drinking beer like it was going out of style, they were covering for me in ways they never even realized they could before.

The Brotherhood of the Bottle

I said I never went to work drunk. That's true. If I was too drunk or hungover or sick from the night before, my wife or even one of my kids would call in sick for me.

That was okay. It was a small plant and word got around. Everyone knew what it meant if a guy's wife called him in sick. With a wink-wink and a nudge-nudge, your supervisor just got off the phone and called someone else in. Hey, I'd done it for them plenty of times.

Now it was their turn.

Sometimes I might be late to work, downing coffee and antacids to try to sober up or get rid of last night's indulgence. That was okay. My friends made sure I never did anything they wouldn't do—or that I'd regret or could possibly get fired from.

And why not? I'd done it for them a hundred times before. These were my guys; they took care of me like I'd taken care of them. We covered for each other, looked out for one another. I didn't want those guys to do anything stupid or lose their job the same way they didn't want me to lose mine because of one too many drinks the night before—or even that morning.

We took turns looking out for each other. And it was a great relationship, the best kind, in fact. I understand my pals on the line the same way they understood me.

My wife? She couldn't understand me. She was too concerned about me to understand. My kids? They were too young, too naive, too innocent. My guys who weren't in the industry, on the job, or on the floor? They didn't get it.

Only these guys, only my guys got it, and we'd all fight fiercely to protect one another. It was a brotherhood of sorts, a brotherhood of the bottle, and it got me through a lot of tough times back in the day.

I like to say that back then I had two jobs: my day job and my drinking. When I wasn't drinking, I was thinking about drinking. When I wasn't thinking about drinking, I was making excuses for my drinking, sleeping off a drunk, getting ready for a bender, or finagling to cover a shift so I could drink or not show up already drunk. It really was like a full-time job.

As you can imagine, working two jobs didn't leave much time for my family. They gave and I took; it was as simple as that. They gave their time, their energy, their love, and their understanding, and I took the time all that bought me to drink more or get over drinking more.

None of us were saints, of course. You can't live with an alcoholic and not get frustrated from time to time. There were fights, and rifts, and alliances forged and broken. There were empty promises on my part, and anger and resentment on theirs.

And who could blame them? Ask anyone who's ever tried it, and you may know a little bit about what I'm talking about here yourself; living with a drunk is never easy.

Sometimes it's close to impossible. It's like living next to a black hole; it's nearly impossible not to get sucked into their sickness, even if you've never touched a drop of alcohol. There would be fights and flare-ups, locked doors, and plenty of nights passed out on the couch.

I would apologize, make excuses and explanations and promise after promise. Well, of course, I would lie, deny, and alibi—that was my unofficial motto for half my life. To show my good faith and remorsefulness, I'd quit drinking for a day or two, a weekend or two, maybe even a whole month.

"Cleaning up my act," I'd call it.

"Waiting for the inevitable" is probably closer to how my family felt about these tenuous and uncertain and inevitably short-lived times. But I was trying. I'd do the dutiful husband thing. We'd get a sitter and have dinner and a movie, all without a single drop. And I'd rediscover my wife and our relationship all over again.

I'd take the girls camping in the backyard or to the arcade or putt-putt, just a daddy-daughters day, and their laughter and smiles and forgiveness would remind me how precious being a father could be.

But in the end, it was never enough. Friday night would creep around, or a Sunday cookout featuring a cooler full of ice-cold beer just calling my name. That would be it for my so-called sobriety, and the vicious cycle would start all over again.

Amazingly, with all that was at stake during this time of my life—my marriage, my kids, the house, the cars, the job, the pension, the security—the thought of simply *not drinking* never occurred to me. The height of an alcoholic's sickness is when the booze literally consumes their life to the point where it becomes the center of their universe.

That's how it got for me. I'd move heaven and earth; call in every favor I'd ever earned; abuse every family member or friend; lie, deny, and alibi just to avoid *not* drinking. It seems ridiculous, pathological, even suicidal to me now. Back then it was just another Tuesday.

Reasons or Excuses?

Very few people start drinking for no good reason. In fact, I've never met a drunk alive who didn't have a good reason—hell, who didn't have a few *dozen* good reasons—for why they were sitting there next to me at the bar drinking:

- "I drink because of the pressure of the job."
- "I drink because I don't have a job."
- "I drink because I lost my job."
- "I drink because my wife is always nagging me."
- "I drink because my ex-wife is always nagging me."
- "I drink because my new wife is always nagging me."
- "I drink because I don't have a wife…"

These aren't reasons, they're excuses. Hear this: the only reason an alcoholic drinks, ever, is to get drunk. You don't pick up a drink if you don't want to alter your current state in some form or fashion.

Some just need to alter it a little, others a lot, while others need to drink so much they have to move to another state completely, but the real reason alcoholics drink is to get drunk. Period.

What was my reason? I wanted, I needed to get drunk, case closed. Ever since that first college dance when that beautiful girl danced with me, I had been hooked. I knew that every success I had, every goal I'd reached, every failure I'd avoided since then was all thanks to drinking.

Drinking made me feel strong and powerful, superior and super, all in one; I was an instant superhero—just add alcohol. It's like the way guys will develop an attachment to a jersey they wore that time their favorite team won a game.

Suddenly it's all that jersey's fault. It's their lucky jersey. The team will lose, the season will be ruined, the sky will fall if they don't wear that jersey to that stadium to support that team. Nothing else will do, but they keep it in pristine condition and heaven help them if they lose it.

Alcohol was my lucky…everything. I could no longer function without it, and I was certain that if I stopped for good, my whole world would crumble. Little did I know, that was about to happen anyway.

CHAPTER 5

How NOT to Be a Survivor

After the hospital, after the burn unit, after the rehab, when I was supposed to be in the clear, I saw my darkest hours fall instead. It wasn't just the booze and the lying and the running around that was tearing me down; it was the blame. Oh, don't get me wrong. I didn't blame myself. (Not yet, anyway.)

Instead, I blamed everyone else for my accident.

Despite all the evidence to the contrary, I blamed, in no particular order, Exxon, for not changing out those valves sooner; my coworkers, for not riding my butt harder about safety; my family, just because they were easy targets; God, for just about anything and everything; the drunk priest who'd fumbled my last rites; the folks at rehab who kept telling me I had to push harder, harder; and the doctors who kept telling me I had to have just one more operation.

In fact, just about the only person I didn't blame for my accident was...myself.

I was one angry, mad, selfish, blaming SOB. By this point I was working at Exxon again, in charge of safety no less, but that wasn't going any better than anything else in my life.

Frankly, I got no respect at work. I always figured it was because folks around the plant thought I was a joke, a clown who'd nearly cost them their jobs while the refinery had been shut down to clean up my mess.

In reality, I didn't respect myself, and they knew it. They knew I was just there collecting a paycheck and killing time until I could go drink again. What's worse, I knew it as well.

We kind of had this begrudging relationship, the guys at the plant and I. The unwritten message was, "You keep yelling, Charlie, and we'll keep ignoring you. Trust us, we know what we're doing. Not like you…"

For a time, it worked. At home, things weren't quite so clear-cut. My wife resented the fact that after all I'd been through, I was right back to square one: working too much, drinking too much, never around for her and the kids.

The kids? I know they resented me as well. I tried to buy their love with things—riding lessons and sailboat rides and concert tickets and clothes—but they didn't want things. They wanted their dad, but Dad couldn't be there for them. Not emotionally, anyway. And on all those long nights or weekends at the bar? I guess not physically as well.

And still I was angry. What did they want from me? Didn't they know the pain I'd been through? Couldn't they see the scars? I was working, wasn't I? Paying the bills, taking good care of them? What did they care if I drowned my sorrows at the bar every night?

But I knew I couldn't keep living that way. It got to the point finally where I had to face facts. Either I wake up, grow up, and face up to taking responsibility for my own actions, good or bad, or I might as well just end it all. At the time, ending it all seemed like the best idea I had.

Booze, pills, anger, melancholy, tears, and curses couldn't quench the demons howling inside. And don't think I didn't try all of the above, sometimes every day. One day I found myself sitting in my mother's basement with a shotgun pointed at my head, ready to end it all.

After all I'd been through, after all I'd done to survive, I couldn't believe I'd gotten to this point. Me? Of all people? Cool Charlie, the macho man? I'd never understood guys who committed suicide. It never made sense to me. To me, that was the easy way out, the coward's way.

It seemed like such a selfish act, the kind that let the victim out of all the responsibility and left the family having to deal with everything: the cleanup, the funeral, the will, the fallout, the memories, the loss, the loneliness. The victim gets out of all the pain; the family left behind gets to feel twice as much.

So tell me, what kind of man does that to his family?

Then again, I supposed, suicide was a lot like drinking. I got to escape the pain and the misery every night, but my wife, my kids, my parents had to watch me make a fool of myself, watch me get arrested or stumble in, messing myself and passing out on the couch.

I wondered, how was suicide any different from that?

"Because Charlie," I told myself that day, "this is permanent."

I paused to look around the basement filled with warm, familiar mementos of my innocent youth. I looked at the family photos of happier times, the boxes of holiday decorations, and the knickknacks Mom was so proud of.

My parents had been so good to me my entire life. They'd been nothing but kind, generous, and thoughtful. So what the hell was I doing here? In their home? With this gun? In these hands? Why had I come here of all places?

Just because my dad was the only one I knew with a gun? Had I gotten that lazy? Or was there more to it? I couldn't have picked up a Saturday night special for a few bills at some pawnshop and driven to some remote stretch and done it there? At least then some random citizen or state trooper or patrolman would find me and not my poor mother.

What would it look like? I wondered, my hands trembling on the stock of my father's shotgun. *How long would it take to clean up? How much would it cost?*

I guess, at that point, I just didn't care. There was no one more important to me than my mother, and if I was willing to put her through the shock and horror of finding her own son in the basement, his head blown off, blood everywhere, then I had to be pretty damn low-down.

And I was about as low as you could go. No, I wasn't low so much as I was just...plain...*numb*; that was it. Numb. Like I'd already died and just didn't know it. Like I'd had so much pain in my life, physical and mental, my nerve endings were flat-out worn down.

There were no real highs in my life anymore, no real lows, either, just a greasy black dread, a kind of tired, cold numbness. I went here, I went there, and none of it mattered much. I didn't taste the beer I drank, didn't so much chew the food I ate as much as gulp it down because my stomach said, "Feed me."

The only two emotions I even felt anymore were self-pity and anger, so why bother punishing everyone I'd loved with *them*? Hadn't they already had enough?

Hadn't *I*?

The shotgun felt cold in my hands. Like the days I'd dragged through ever since the accident, it felt long and black and cold. Despite my long sleeves—I always wore long sleeves now—I could see the hints of my scars poking out just above the cuff as I struggled to shift the gun into place. They disgusted me. Life disgusted me. I disgusted me.

And yet here I was, finger on the trigger, barrel cold against my forehead and...what? I couldn't do it. I was hesitating, giving myself time to chicken out, to get cold feet. And I did. Fortunately, at the last minute, I didn't have the guts to pull the trigger.

I sat and thought about my life, about what I'd already done to my family and what this would do to them as well. The tough guy turned out to be not so tough after all. Or maybe (or hopefully) smarter than he thought.

Either way, the thought of my poor mother finding me

that way in her basement, in my childhood home with my brain on her walls, and what that would do to her after all she'd already been through stopped me cold.

I put the gun away and never said a word about what I'd almost done on that bleak, dismal day. Only years later, speaking to audiences around the country, would I have the courage to fess up about what I'd almost done. I'd never had the courage to tell my own mother, but it felt easy to tell total strangers. At least that way, I could show them that suicide is real, that it wears a human face, and that even tough guys think about doing it.

I wish I could say that was the last time I attempted to take my life. Unfortunately, it was only the first…

Rock Bottom? It Was Just the Beginning

You would think that blowing up an entire refinery and endangering my life and the lives of everyone around me would at last be rock bottom for a guy. That destroying his life and the lives of his family would be enough to say, "Enough is enough."

You would think that, and in my case, you'd be wrong.

For me in my sickness, the accident was literally just the beginning of a whole new level of drinking. If you thought I drank before the refinery fire, look out.

And why not? If I thought I was under pressure before, try now. If I thought my family dynamic was strained before I burned 50 percent of my body, try now. If I thought

I felt insecure and like a failure before being covered with scars, try now.

Now? I was in pain, emotionally, physically. I drank to bury the pain, I drank to forget the pain, I drank to forget I was drinking to bury the pain. There was no vicious cycle because cycles have a beginning and an end. This was more like a vicious whirlwind that never stopped and never started; it simply...was.

Two Kinds of Therapy

Obviously, they weren't pumping me full of alcohol in the emergency room that night or even in the Burn Center for weeks, then months afterward. But I couldn't have had a drink then even if I'd wanted to. I was in a kind of medical, physical, emotional, and spiritual limbo.

I was also pretty much a captive. The only places I went during that time were downstairs to the debriding tanks and upstairs to my room. And even in my first therapy center, I was still an inpatient. So there was a period of close to half a year that I call my "forced sobriety." Where I didn't drink simply because I couldn't drink.

I mean physically I couldn't get my hands on a drink.

But once I was released and began my therapy on an outpatient basis months after the accident, look out. And even though I was on a rigid schedule of physical therapy, that only took up my days. That left my nights free so I could take up a second form of therapy: alcohol therapy.

By day I sweated and cried and strained at the physical therapist's office; by night I was practicing alcohol therapy at the nearest bar. It was dark, everyone knew me, everyone knew what had happened, and no one asked any questions. They all bought me drinks. I felt safe there, and at this point, I needed safety more than anything else.

If I'd thought things would change after the accident, on the home front, I mean, I'd been wrong. My family was sympathetic to a point. They'd seen the scars, they'd heard the screams, they'd felt my tears, they knew what I'd been through.

But it hadn't been easy for them, either. How'd you like to go to the grocery store and have everyone whispering behind your back about "the wife of the guy who blew up the Exxon plant"? Or go to school and hear the rumors about your dad and why he'd been so careless.

But I didn't know any of that then. All I knew was that I was in pain, and the only thing that could drown it was alcohol. I was on leave from the plant, but it was a paid leave. So not only was I providing for my family while in therapy—physical, alcohol, or otherwise—but also we were doing damn well.

The bills were still getting paid. We still had our house, the two-car garage, the two cars, so...what were they complaining about? What did my family want from me?

Sure, I was drowning my sorrows. Sure, I was feeling sorry for myself. And no, alcohol wasn't the answer; never could be, never would be. But who was I hurting? If I was hurting anyone, I was only hurting myself.

Meanwhile, I thought my family wanted for nothing. My wife could go to lunch with her friends, shop wherever, whenever she wanted, and all I asked for was a little time after my therapy to drown my sorrows. Was that so bad?

My daughters had everything they could want and then some. If they wanted to go sailing, I rented them a boat. If they wanted to go horseback riding, I rented them horses. If they wanted to go to a concert, I paid for the tickets.

So why couldn't my family leave me alone? Well, they couldn't leave me alone because they were still acting like we were a family, while I was acting like they were a nuisance.

My wife didn't want to go to lunch with her friends. She'd just spent six months eating cafeteria food while I was in the burn unit and then rehab; she wanted to eat with her husband. My kids didn't want to go on pony rides and sailboats alone; they wanted their dad.

And all I wanted was another drink. All I cared about was another drink. I needed to drink to drown out the memory of the sound of the flames consuming my skin, to drown out the sound of the screams in those debriding tanks or that poor kid crying himself to sleep every night in our room.

My wife wanted a husband, and my kids wanted a father. They wanted me there with them, but I couldn't be there with them, not physically and certainly not emotionally.

All my wife's accomplishments, her hopes, her fears, her worries and regrets fell on deaf ears. I missed my kids' concerts and plays and games and talent shows and awards and field days and more all because I was too busy sitting in some bar somewhere, drowning my sorrows.

I couldn't even be there for my father on his deathbed. Now, here was a man who'd never missed a single one of my sporting events, not one. The man worked two jobs, sometimes three, his entire life to provide for his family, and still he found time to cheer me on from the sidelines. And if he couldn't find time, he made time.

He went without so that my brother and I could have the best scooters on the street, the best gloves on the sandlot, the best birthdays on the block. After my accident and his subsequent stroke, my father deteriorated rapidly.

When he was on his deathbed, even though I knew he was close to the end, I slipped out to grab a quick drink at the corner bar. One drink became two, and two became three. By the time I got back to the hospital, I knew it was too late.

I saw my brother, Jerry, holding my father's hand; my brother saw me. Simply, almost stoically, he said two words and no more: "Dad's died." The man who'd been there for me for everything in life passed away only looking at one son. While he was sucking in his last breath, I was around the corner, in a bar, sucking down one last beer.

I just couldn't help it. There was so much to feel, and I didn't want to feel any of it. That was what the alcohol was for; it numbed the pain. But it also numbed my soul.

Strike Two

Not long after my father died, I got my second drunk-driving ticket. This one was even worse because I got it right in front of my mother's house. I could see her standing on the porch, wringing her hands.

"Why?" she asked through her tears as the cops hauled me away once more to the drunk tank. "Charlie, why?"

Since this was strike number two for Cool Charlie, it was very, very strongly suggested—and worded—that I take an alcohol education class. Of course, I did. Not to learn anything about alcohol. I knew all there was to know about that, trust me. But to scrub the points from my ticket, to get everyone off my back, not only the state of New Jersey, but also my mother, my daughters, and my wife as well.

As I sat there in class with the rest of the repeat offenders, I knew that I had to quit drinking once and for all. If it wasn't quite rock bottom, it simply made sense: next time there'd be no second chance—I'd get thrown in jail.

So I quit drinking again. Cold turkey again. This time it was for good. Or so I thought. I even tested myself, sitting in the same bars, with the same crowd, during the same "second therapy" hours as before. Nothing had really changed at all, except for the fact that while they drank a beer or a shot or a glass of scotch or rum, I sipped at a glass of club soda.

It felt strange; it didn't fit. I thought I'd feel better, prouder, but I didn't. All I felt was adrift. I was a man with no country. I didn't fit in with the barflies, who couldn't understand why I'd quit drinking and yet still came to the bar. And I didn't fit in with my family, who I believed were just waiting for me to fall off the wagon.

They weren't alone.

Ain't Life Grand

Though I may have felt out of sync between a drink and a hard place, I started to feel better. My scars were starting to heal, and the therapy was paying off. So was alcohol class; I got my driver's license back. I was spending less time at the bar and more with my family. All in all, life was looking up.

Then Exxon sent me to attend a safety school in—of all places—Las Vegas. I was pretty stoked. Not only was I back at work, but after all we'd been through together, Exxon was actually grooming me for a promotion.

So I checked into my hotel, the MGM Grand. And I'm walking through the lobby on the way to my room when I passed by the bar. It called to me. It looked so appealing, with its bottles and barstools and neon lights, and I thought to myself, pausing in front, *You know, I'm probably not an alcoholic.* I mean, maybe it wasn't the alcoholism driving me to drink. Jesus, you get blown up in a refinery fire and see if you don't drink! Maybe it was just the pain, the scars, the tragedy, the guilt, the remorse, the memories driving me to drink. So why not…test that theory? And so I did. I sat down at that bar in the MGM Grand and never looked back.

I was there for a week; that's how long safety school lasted. And in that week, I proved beyond a shadow of doubt that I was, indeed, an alcoholic. And not just an alcoholic, but a full-blown—my life isn't worth a plug nickel—drunk.

Remember how proud I was not to be a Bowery bum, passing out and blacking out and throwing his life away? That week, I went even the worst Bowery bum one better! I laid in the gutter and had to be helped up. I almost got arrested. I should have been fired for not doing my job, for not even trying. I did all of those things and then some. It was clear to me, if I'd ever had a doubt, I was a regular, garden variety drunk.

Alcoholism is a progressive disease. In many ways, in fact, it's like an elevator that goes in only one direction: down. Now, you can get off that elevator at any floor and still get help. But not me, I had to go all the way to bottom, ground-floor basement level, before I even knew I was taking the ride.

You know that pain I described earlier? The pain of being burned over 50 percent of my body? I never, not in a million years, thought that I could ever endure something like that again. I did, only it was ten times worse.

The agony I felt that week in Vegas, the sheer emotional pain I felt sitting at that bar, day after day, night after night, was worse than the pain I felt in the hospital the night of my accident. Worse even than the pain in the debriding tanks, with bleach and water searing my raw nerve endings shut.

I didn't want to drink, and yet I had to drink. I literally, sincerely could not stop myself, although I tried in the most permanent way imaginable. I can vividly remember standing in front of my window on the twenty-seventh floor of the MGM Grand, struggling with the window to get it open. Why? So I could jump out of it, plain and simple.

There's a reason they seal those windows—so guys like me can't end it all in the depths of severe depression. I have no memory of how I got home from the MGM Grand after the long, seemingly endless week of debauchery.

I do remember leaving the hotel. And on my way out, the doorman of the MGM Grand, a guy who's seen it all and then some, a full-time employee in Sin City, said to me, "Man, I've never seen anyone that drunk in my entire life."

Now, you've got to really top yourself to impress this guy, but I did it.

It Felt Good to Feel Bad

Coming home from Vegas felt like crawling out of a sewer; I'd never been that low in my life. I've been in some low places, but this time I knew I needed help. Not self-help, not from friends and neighbors, not from enablers who meant well but hadn't seen me desperate to jump from the twenty-seventh floor of the MGM Grand.

This time I needed help from the experts, from folks who had been through it and come out the other end. I found a program, and I made it work. The program's not important; the work is. Whatever works for you works. That's my take.

Twelve steps, a church group, tough love, intake, rehab, outpatient, whatever—find a program and stick to it. That's what works; that's the only thing that works. And every day, I worked.

I worked harder at getting sober than I have in just about anything else in my life. I screamed, I cursed, I fought, I cried, I ached to have a drink, but I did the work. I stuck to it, and this time it worked.

It was a long, hellish climb out of that pit, but I made it just the same. And this time the pain wasn't self-inflicted. Now when I hurt, it was because I was supposed to hurt. I was no longer hurting myself.

My mother passed away while I was in recovery, and I was there for her. I was at her side night and day, and she knew it. I wouldn't miss another opportunity to let someone know I was there for them until the very end. And when she passed, I was there at her side, her hand in mine.

I hadn't skipped out to the corner bar for a drink, and while I was grieving, it also felt good; it felt good to feel bad. Just to feel, period. For so long now, decades, it seemed, I'd worked so hard not to feel anything.

That's what alcohol is, really, emotional anesthesia. You take it to feel nothing, and it works every time. Now I was an open wound, but I didn't care. Let the emotions come, let the feelings come, let the pain and the tears and the fears come. I may not have been ready for them, but I was no longer running away, either.

I handled my mother's death in a way I hadn't been prepared to handle my father's. Maybe to make up for the way I'd failed with him, I insisted on taking care of all of it. I took care of the funeral arrangements, of picking out the food for the wake. I took care of the will and the expenses that death brings.

Then it was over: the handling, the phone calls, the kind words, and the details were done. And I had to face facts—my parents were gone. It was just me and my brother now; that was all that was left.

And I felt strangely abandoned. Not in any purposeful way, but in a powerfully emotional way. I could see the warning signs, and I could feel the anxiety pressing against my chest every time I thought of a certain and swift cure: a drink.

I told my wife and kids I needed to get away from the stress, the pain of my mother's passing. I just couldn't take driving around, passing all the places my parents had taken me growing up, the ice cream parlor and the toy store and the movie theater.

I decided to go into the city, to Manhattan, to see some plays and just take my mind off things. They agreed. "Good idea, honey." And the minute I got into the city, I knew it had all been an excuse. I didn't know what plays were showing or which I might be interested in. I just knew I needed to run away, straight into the arms of my old friend alcohol.

I immediately called some of my sponsors in the program and fessed up to my emotions. Each one said the same thing: "You need to get to a meeting, Charlie—and fast."

They found one for me on Forty-second Street. I hurried there, feeling desperate. I found exactly what you'd expect to find at a meeting on Forty-second Street in New York City: the place smelled like urine, people who were actively drinking sat on the steps, and my first instinct was to turn around, to run, to flee and find the nearest bar.

But I wouldn't, I couldn't. I walked up the stairs past those people and found the meeting room. I sat down, clinging to my chair but ready to bolt at any second. And not long after I got there, a guy came over to me. A big guy with missing teeth and wild eyes, his ear looking like someone had been gnawing on it. He had the look of a stray cat, a street look, and he honed right in on me.

He said, "How long do you have in the program?"

What he meant was, of course, "How long have you been clean and sober?"

I answered, "Almost two years."

A crooked grin passed across his weathered face. "You'll do" was all he said.

"I'll do for what?"

"To speak," he said, and promptly walked away.

That was it; I was sunk. You learn quickly that when you're getting sober and someone asks you to do something, you do it; that's just the way it is.

I groaned and I grumbled and then started mumbling, I thought, to myself, "I can't believe this guy just asked me to speak. What the hell am I going to say to these people?"

But I wasn't mumbling to myself, I guess; I was mumbling out loud. And the guy in front of me turned around and said, "Hey, do you know who that was who just asked you to speak?"

I thought it might be some celebrity, some Manhattan hotshot. But the man said, "That was God asking you to speak. He just looks like one of us."

And I knew exactly what he meant. So I stood, and I opened my mouth and started speaking. It was the first time I'd done that at a meeting, and it all came out about my mother's passing, my emotions, what I felt and was thinking, and how badly I wanted a drink.

And these people, rough and street looking as they were, said the warmest, kindest, most genuine things to me. They shared their own struggles, heartaches, failures, and losses. And as we spoke to each other, for each other, I realized I'm no better or worse than them.

Sure, I might have gotten off the elevator and sought help a little sooner, and I might have had some better breaks in life than they had, but their pain was mine. We were feeling the exact same things.

Always the Last to Know

It was a moment of sudden and pure clarity. I got it now. Sitting there surrounded by people I normally would have crossed the street to avoid, I got it. I was a drunk. There were no more excuses, no more lies, denials, or alibis. My clothes might have been a little nicer, my shoes a little cleaner, but this was what people saw when they looked at me—a drunk.

It had taken me so many wasted years to come to that conclusion. I had missed completely what the whole world saw when they looked in my bleary eyes, when they found me wearing the same outfit two days in a row, when they accepted a ride and had to kick empty beer cans off the floor under the passenger seat to find room for their shoes: a drunk.

And I knew it was true what they said in the program: the alcoholic is always the last to *know* they're an alcoholic. Family, friends, neighbors, coworkers, bosses, strangers on the street, even little kids can spot a drunk a mile away, but he's the last to look in the mirror and see his true self.

But I wasn't alone. The scary thing is, at any one time in this country, there are ten million people just like me out there. That's one out of every twenty to twenty-five people in this country who have an alcohol problem.

Doctors, lawyers, priests, secretaries, mothers, fathers, wives, husbands, teachers, and probation officers who don't know they're an alcoholic even though everyone around them has known probably for years.

Running to Stand Still (But without a Drink in My Hand)

After that I tried running away from my problems. I took a little me time, took a little money and traveled all over the country. Clichéd as it sounds, I was literally searching for myself as I wandered the country, letting the road take me where it would, no plan or schedule or even a road map to guide me. Having worked for so long in one spot, day in and day out for thirty years, it was pure freedom to be at loose ends and on the move at last.

At the time I didn't know what I was looking for, but today I can say that I found God again at Yosemite National Park of all places. Having lived in Jersey all my life, and nothing against the Garden State, I found Yosemite the most beautiful place I had ever seen. Somewhere in all that natural beauty, I came to grips with the biggest problem in my life: me.

I barely felt the scars that covered my arms and back as I climbed all the way up to a lookout spot called Glacier Point. The view from on high was spectacular, offering an expansive panorama of many of Yosemite's greatest features, such as the famous Yosemite Falls.

In a word, it was breathtaking.

For a guy used to driving the same ten minutes to work and back every day, it was like visiting a whole other planet, one that had yet to be taken over by oil and machines and ugly scaffolding and miles of endless pipeline.

I stood there and the beauty of the place brought me to tears. For the first time in my life, I began to see things clearly. There is a God, and it was divine intervention that had saved my life after all.

He had put the drunk priest in the hospital that day. It was all according to *his* plan. Whether he knew it or not, that priest saved my life. I agree that it's not your normal type of miracle, not the clean-cut Hollywood type with bright lights and harps playing, but I believe that's exactly what it was—a miracle. He put me on the road to seeing myself as I was, and that person needed a lot of help.

Of course, we all have to come down off the mountaintop sometime, and that's when grim reality sets back in. As usual, the view from below wasn't quite so pretty.

The View from Below

If this were a movie, there'd be happy, triumphant music playing right now—you know the kind I'm talking about, maybe even *Rocky* music—to let you know this is where the happy ending starts.

Well, unfortunately, that happy ending wasn't always so happy, and for an alcoholic, you never quite cross the finish line. Instead, you take it as the saying goes, "day by day." And that's exactly what I did. Some days were good, others were bad, but each one was sober, for the most part—except when they weren't, and then I had to start the process all over again.

In fact, I spent a lot more time *getting* sober than *being* sober. I worked the program and I worked it well. After the experience on Forty-second Street, I found that I had a knack for speaking to alcoholics. What's more, I wanted to.

I wanted them to feel my pain, I wanted to feel theirs, and above all, I wanted us to work together to find the healing we all needed. I began speaking to audiences on the subject of addiction and accepting responsibility. The more I spoke, the better I felt. The more I helped, the less I wanted to hurt. Through helping others, I was finally able to heal myself.

Eventually I was asked to speak at an alcohol and rehabilitation hospital. When I arrived to give my presentation that day, the first person I saw at the hospital was, you guessed it, the drunk priest.

He wasn't a patient—he ran the hospital! (And he was no longer a drunk, either.) Pulling me aside after my presentation, the priest told me that after he was told what he had said to me that day, he was so guilt ridden that he sought help for his own problems.

Just as he had saved my life, I had saved his.

Imagine that. The man I had wanted to kill so badly, and who wanted me to die so quickly, had been my savior, and what's more, I had been his. We had a common path to follow now, and that was to accept responsibility for our own lives and hopefully help other people accept responsibility for theirs.

I had found my calling, if you will, and that calling was safety.

Life Begins with Sobriety

I had a saying during my drinking days: "If you can't drink, you might as well die." I really believed that. Drinking was the only way I felt anything in those days, even if all I felt was pain, guilt, shame, misery, and failure. It was better, I figured, than feeling nothing at all.

I always believed that I'd survive the drinking, even survive the accident, but die of what I called "terminal boredom." I really believed that drinking was where it was at, that anyone who didn't drink just didn't get it, that they must be the most boring people and lead the most boring lives on earth.

But I'm here to tell you that after fourteen years of sobriety, I am now an active participant in my life again; and it's thrilling. Every day sober is a new adventure. I feel everything—the good, the bad, the ugly, and everything in between.

When my daughters call me, I'm there to pick up the phone, and they know it. When my wife hugs me, I feel every nerve ending and thank God I can. When friends give me good news, I'm genuinely happy for them. When I can connect with an audience and touch people's lives, oh, man, it's an electric feeling that puts anything I ever felt under the influence to shame.

I was an expert in the art of lie, deny, and alibi. No longer. Today I openly and actively communicate with everyone I come into contact with; I am alive and aware and respect all people and their opinions.

I have met so many of you on my journeys around the country speaking about safety. In boardrooms and back rooms, in convention centers and hotel ballrooms, at ball fields and on factory floors, I am never short of amazed at the vibrant diversity of life I come into contact with.

Every one of us has a story, and I'm eager and ready to hear as many as I can before I die. I think of all the things

I missed while I was drinking—all the award ceremonies, the birthday dinners, the volleyball games, and talent shows and graduations and phone calls and movies and popcorn and late-night talks.

What could I have said to my daughters to make their lives easier, rather than harder, while growing up?

How could I have celebrated my wife's achievements and shared her pain, her hopes, her fears, and her joys?

What might I have said to my father as he lay there dying to make his journey to the other side easier? What wisdom might he have imparted before he left if only I'd been there—and not at the corner bar with a shot and a beer—to hear it?

To say I have regrets is to say an alcoholic has excuses. In other words, I have a million of them! My regrets alone could fill the pages of an entire book or a dozen whole books.

But I'm not here to look back anymore; I'm here to look forward. Back when I was drinking, my family loved to go to the beach. My beautiful wife, my lovely daughters, and I would sit there and watch the sun go down on another long, sunny day.

And my wife would say, "Look at that beautiful sunset."

And I'd say, "Yeah, that's beautiful. Hand me another beer."

To the alcoholic me, a glorious sunset was just another excuse to down the next six-pack and let my wife drive me home again. Today when I see a sunset, whether I'm with my family or flying home from another seminar or just looking out my hotel room over another strange city, I say, "Thank you, God, for another amazing day!"

If you're an alcoholic or you're living with an alcoholic or working with one or troubling over one or making excuses for one, you are missing out on all your amazing days.

The worst part about my disease was not what I did to myself, but what I did to so many, many people whom I love and cherish to this day. An alcoholic may drink alone, but he doesn't live in a vacuum.

His actions affect everyone around him from the bartender he abuses to the wife he ignores to the kids he never sees to the other folks on the road as he swerves his way back from yet another bar. And if you're drinking on the job or allowing others to drink on the job, you're putting the entire plant at risk.

The harsh words of a drunk—even the alcoholic who ignores or neglects his family without actively or physically hurting them—leaves scars that never, ever heal. I know because I've scarred so many people in my life.

I robbed my first wife of a meaningful, giving, respectful relationship. I robbed my daughters of their childhood, and in many ways I'm watching them cope with that lost childhood even as they struggle—and I do mean struggle—to become functioning adults. I robbed my mother of her son, my brother of his best friend, and my father of our last few moments together. I can never get those moments back—not with my father, my mother, or any of my family.

I can work hard to regain their trust, and I have every day of my sobriety, but there's a gulf there that's impossible to bridge. I can't imagine what I said or did to them in my drunken moments, the ones I no longer remember but that they will never forget.

"Son, I'm Proud of You."

Despite all the pain I've caused and felt because of the accident and my alcoholism, today I consider myself a most fortunate person. Not because of the beautiful house I live in, or the professional success I'm experiencing, or the trips I get to take all over the world speaking to good folks like you.

I'm fortunate because I've got a second chance in life. A second chance to live right and make things right. And every time I write one word in a book like this or speak to another few hundred employees at an industrial plant or warehouse or refinery or pipeline, I'm thrilled to be able to share some of my good fortune, even some of my hard-earned wisdom, with you.

Because I owe it to you. For every person I hurt in my life, I've vowed to make a positive impression on someone else. For every wrong that I've done, and there have been so many, I've vowed to make things right.

I can't go back in time and undo the scars I've given my family, my friends, my loved ones, my coworkers, my supervisors, and even random strangers. All I can do is move forward every day and live right.

The proudest day of my life was not when Exxon made me safety supervisor of my old plant, or when I learned I had the highest-selling safety video in the country, or even when I started my own company.

The proudest day of my life can be summed up in five short words. My mother said them to me on her deathbed. The things I hadn't been able to do for my father, I tried desperately to do for my mother.

I visited her around the clock. I cared for her, fed her, listened to her, sat there while she slept. And I was there when she died. And sick as she was, this woman who'd wrung her hands and hung her head in shame every time she saw me out in public and drunk again, she summoned her last breath to tell me this: "Son, I'm proud of you."

If you're struggling with your own sobriety or enabling someone who is struggling with theirs, if this is the first time you've ever been told to stop enabling an alcoholic or to stop letting others enable you, then I'd rather it be me than some cop on the other side of the drunk tank bars, or worse, some state trooper telling you that you've just blindsided a bus full of kids on their way to a soccer game.

If my words have in any way persuaded you to take the first step toward getting help for yourself, a loved one, or a coworker, then let me be the first one to say to you, "I'm proud of you."

It won't be easy; it never is. But it's worth it. It has to be because you have no other choice. If you don't get help for yourself, it's your life that's in danger. If you don't get help for someone else, it's their life and the lives of everyone around them that could be at risk.

The way I see it, neither one is an option...

CHAPTER 6

My Definition of Safety

My daughters. God, how I love them. And I don't know how two girls can be as different as my two girls and still be sisters, but they are. Jennifer, the youngest, is as outgoing as her old man. Dana, my older daughter, is as quiet and sensitive as they come.

When I first started giving my presentations and talked openly about my daughters, I used to say that Jennifer was too young to be affected by the accident, that she was fine.

But Jennifer wasn't fine; she was far from it. Recently, in fact, she started therapy as a direct result of the baggage she has left over from those years I was in recovery and then struggling as a result of the accident.

I guess she wasn't fine after all.

And poor Dana, my eldest and most sensitive girl, went from being a straight-A student at the time of the accident to failing all her classes, and years later, a suicide attempt finally exposed her own emotional scars from her painful childhood.

Everything I had I lost. Everything my family had they lost. We lost each other and are still trying to put the pieces back together. Father, mother, husband, wife, daughters—all our paths were tragically altered, now and forever, by a single split-second decision I made to ignore proper protocol, safety goggles, or flame-retardant gear.

To be macho, to be quick, to be lazy—and look at what it cost me, what it cost us.

You know my biggest fear these days? It's that reading this book or seeing one of my presentations, you or the guy or the gal next to you will sit back, breathe a sigh of relief, and say, "Well, thank God, that'll never happen to me. I don't work at a chemical plant. I don't work at a refinery. I don't have a dangerous job."

Hear this: the job I did—the location, the job description, the chemicals, and the plant—had nothing, absolutely nada to do with my accident. I caused my accident. What causes every home or workplace accident is our own personal **attitude about safety.**

I caused my accident, plain and simple.

The choice was always up to me, and it's always up to you.

So much of what happened to me was avoidable; that's what hurts so much. Hurts more than the scars and the pain and the sunlight on my skin. If I had worn sleeves on my flame-retardant clothing, my arms wouldn't have been scarred.

If I'd worn safety goggles as I was supposed to, I could have seen the clear path to the safety shower. If I'd turned the truck off as I was supposed to, the worst I would have suffered was a chemical burn. Some mild irritation, some physical discomfort, some antibiotics, maybe a trip or two to the dermatologist and I'd be in the clear.

It was my responsibility to follow procedure, and I blew it. And now I'll have to live with it and so will my family. So many of us think it's someone else's job to keep us safe—the CEO, management, the safety board, the manufacturer.

It's our responsibility, first and foremost, to keep ourselves safe, not to rely on others to keep us safe.

Everybody deserves a future.

Don't let it happen to you.

It Starts with Safety

Safety? Why I thought what I thought about safety is a big part of my story. And if you're reading this, it's probably a big part of your story up to now as well. For me, job safety—or the lack of it—was a mind-set, a pattern of behavior that took me years to reverse.

The crazy thing was, I was safe part of the time, but not nearly enough. Take procedure at Exxon. I was, technically speaking, wearing a flame-retardant shirt that night of the accident. Only, me being me, I had rolled up the sleeves since it was a hot and muggy night.

On my arms today, you can literally see where the sleeves

started because they're the only part of my body that *wasn't* burned. It's kind of like when you're wearing a T-shirt and your arms get sunburned. But without the flame-retardant material on my uniform, I know I'd be dead right now.

And I was wrong about another thing, too. The accident didn't just affect me. It might have been 50 percent of *my* body that got burned that summer night back in 1980, but in the process I burned 100 percent of the people that meant the most to me.

In the end, I took a lot of people with me.

Mine is the story of an unimaginable—but looking back, purely inevitable—event that changed my life in a matter of seconds. Just like that, the man I was cracked in two, and somebody else took his place. I was never the same after that and my family wasn't, either.

The accident continued to reshape who I was, how I thought, and what was important to me over the course of the next three decades. Yes, it took that long to become the man I am today. In many ways, I'm still becoming the man I am today.

Hollywood Endings Are for Sissies

We all want what I call Hollywood endings, where the pretty music plays and we walk off into the sunset happily ever after. Or at least, happy for now. But real life isn't quite so simple; it takes longer for change—true change—to take hold.

Whenever I tell people—whether it's an audience or an acquaintance—about the accident, they seem to think that being literally "blown up" was the turning point where I changed my life suddenly and overnight.

But it wasn't, not by a long shot.

I say the accident was inevitable because it was bound to happen. I was setting myself up for it to happen. What's more, it was the outcome of the person I was at the time—the result of a lot of negative behaviors and a state of mind that took many, many years to overcome (well past the five long, painful years I spent in hospitals trying to undo the physical damage I'd caused that night).

The truth is that the real thing that was unsafe in my life at that time was *me*. It wasn't chemicals or protocol or even the hazards of my job. My attitude, my whole approach to life at that point, was wrong.

I was almost dead wrong.

The fallout is not always swift, but it's fairly certain. The ripples from this kind of accident, from any accident, are as invisible as they are inevitable.

And above all, they are intensely, ultimately personal.

Safety Is Personal

Years ago I was speaking to a company in Maine. I was giving my usual speech, telling my usual story, and I noticed a man sitting in a wheelchair in the back of the room.

He was curious and alert as I gave my speech, and I made

it a point to go up to him after I was through speaking and introduce myself. He said his name was Frank.

Frank and I talked for a minute about safety in general and him in particular. Eventually I had to ask, "Frank, how did you wind up in that wheelchair?"

It turns out Frank hadn't been hurt on the job, but at home. He'd been trimming a tree, as so many of us do, on one sunny fall weekend. He wasn't harnessed or roped into the tree at all, just kind of freewheeling. Eventually the chainsaw kicked back, knocked him out of the tree, and he fell to the ground.

Frank severed his spine and was paralyzed from the neck down. When Frank had finished telling me his story, I asked him, "Frank, what's the worst thing about being in that wheelchair?"

Frank looked at me with tears in his eyes and said, "Charlie, you know how some days you come home from work, and your wife is standing with her back to you, washing dishes in the kitchen sink? And you walk up behind her just because and give her a hug?"

I thought of my own wife washing dishes in our kitchen and how when I hugged her all I saw were the scars of my arms. But I knew exactly what he meant. I smiled and said, "Sure, Frank."

"Well, Charlie, what I hate most about being in this wheelchair is that I can't do that anymore."

My Definition of Safety

When it comes to safety, I couldn't have said it any better myself. What's more, safety is no more simple, no more complicated, no more expensive, no more academic, no more personal than Frank's story.

You want to know what safety is, bottom line? I'll tell you exactly what it is: safety, at its most basic, is about going home at night to put your arms around your wife, to kiss your kids, period.

It's about having the right and the responsibility to leave work as safely and in as many pieces as when you clocked in that day or night. It's about the little things: tossing a ball with your kid on the weekend, giving your daughter a high five when she aces her math test.

At its heart, safety is about coming up behind your wife and giving her a hug after a long, tiring shift.

Everything else—numbers, Total Recordable Injury (TRI) reports, paradigm shifts, and incident reports—is secondary to that. You wouldn't think about driving home from work without your seat belt on, right? So how is putting on your safety goggles or Nomex gloves any different? Unfortunately, safety is like a lot of other things—we don't really appreciate or respect it until it's not an option anymore.

The time for me to think about wearing safety goggles was *before* I was doused in chemicals and running past my truck to a safety shower, not *after*. And yet the man I was at the time was too tough for that, too cool.

(Psst, any of this sounding familiar yet?)

Generally speaking, safety is one of those assumptions we make when we get up in the morning. The toaster will work, the coffeemaker won't blow up, the car will start, the printer will have enough ink in the cartridge, and we'll get home safe and sound.

It doesn't always work out that way.

The American Way of Life: Speed First, Safety Second

We are a country of do-it-yourselfers, builders, adventurers, amateur chefs, and home remodelers, and yet we are also Americans. That means we specialize in doing it in half the time, with half the effort—and all before prime time.

According to the Centers for Disease Control (CDC), there are more than twenty-eight million visits to the emergency room every year for "unintentional injuries." (I'm not quite sure how many ER visits there are for *intentional* injuries, but that's probably a great topic for a whole other book!)

Of all the causes of death in this country every year—from heart attacks to strokes to cancer to homicide and other violent crimes—accidental death ranks **fifth on the list**. Fifth. That number represents millions of unnecessary deaths each year, simply because we're putting speed—or other factors like convenience, using the wrong tools, or even inexperience—over safety.

Ten Things Safety Is...

Everyone thinks they know what safety is, but...do we really? Do we know how to use our fire extinguishers, that new miter saw, and oh, by the way, how many spoonfuls of medicine to give the kid when he's sick? And does it have to be children's medicine? (Hell, I had the damndest time finding the hazard lights in our new car!)

While it seems like everything these days—from fast-food coffee cups to shampoo bottles—has a warning label, I'm still amazed by the amount of people who come up to me at functions and list a catalog of their latest household accidents. Mostly that's because what we think is safe generally isn't. That is, when we stop to think of safety in the first place. (Which we usually don't.)

Safety is many things. Here are ten of them:

1. **Safety Is...Simple:** Whatever you're doing, on the job or off, it usually takes from only a few seconds to no more than a few minutes to do it safer. Every plant I've ever toured, every shop floor I've ever spoken on, has safety procedures posted, primed, and ready. It only takes a few moments to go home to your family each night.

2. **Safety Is...Responsible:** You owe it to your employer, your boss, your manager, your family, your friends, your coworkers, your partner(s) to do it

right, to do it well...and to do it safely. Anything less is simply irresponsible.

3. **Safety Is...a Forgotten Art:** I think the first—and last—place I ever heard about safety in school was in shop class! But...what if you didn't take shop? Or what if, like me, you weren't exactly paying attention? In the old days we helped each other build barns, dig ditches, even put up shelves or pave a driveway. Today it is quite literally do-it-yourself. That might mean you're doing things you're not quite qualified to do, unsupervised and quite alone. What if you cut your finger badly with that new miter saw and faint from blood loss before you can reach the phone to call 911 or even get to your neighbor's house? It could be hours before someone finds you; days if you live alone. It's not a horror movie scenario. It happens every day in this country simply because folks don't think it will happen to them.

4. **Safety Is...Mandatory:** The thing about safety is you've got to do it. Period, end of discussion. On the job, it's part of your job description. Even at home, it's part of your job description. At work your coworkers depend on you; at home, it's your family. Are you willing to let either of them down?

5. **Safety Is...Fast:** How long does it take to shut off the circuit breaker before you install that ceiling fan? Ten seconds? Five? How long does it take to familiarize your family once a year with your getaway plan in case of a fire? Or to switch out those fire alarm batteries on New Year's Day?

6. **Safety Is...a Joint Effort:** What I learned about safety from my accident is that safety isn't an isolated incident; it's a collective one. In other words, you fall off the roof while cleaning the gutters, and you put your whole family at risk. Maybe you're out of work for a week, maybe a month...maybe a year. Will your short-term disability cover you for the entire duration? Do you even have short-term disability coverage?

7. **Safety Is...Habitual:** The thing about safety is that it's habitual. In other words, before the accident I was in the habit of ignoring pretty much every safety protocol except for the ones that would get me fired. Afterward, of course, I was all safety, all the time—and still obviously am—and that's my point: Don't let it get to the point where years of rehab and millions of dollars in plastic surgery are what it takes to make you more careful. Start the process now so safety becomes a habit sooner.

8. **Safety Is ... Cheap:** I was pricing fire extinguishers the other day and most of them, the good ones anyway, were between $19.99 and $49.99. And how much is a decent flashlight? Five bucks? Ten? Gloves, goggles, boots, the basics for solid home safety are mighty cheap these days, and for under a hundred bucks in most cases, you can save someone in your family's life or even your own. Do I even have to ask if it's worth it?

9. **Safety Is ... Your Responsibility (Not the Other Guy's):** The thing about safety that we all generally feel is that—well, I don't have to worry about it because someone else already has. But the government isn't going to come into your home and put a fire extinguisher every five hundred feet or monitor you as you wobble on the top step of that rickety old ladder. It's more than just common sense that puts safety first; it's personal responsibility in the hands of each one of us.

10. **Safety Is ... First:** Bottom line, life is one big obstacle course full of ways to get broken, bent, burned, scraped, smashed, snapped, or scalded. For your sake, for your family's sake, put safety first!

Ten Things Safety Isn't . . .

Okay, so we know what safety *is*, but sometimes knowing what something *isn't* is as effective as knowing the truth. Here are some frequent misconceptions about safety that I'd like to clear up now:

1. **Safety Isn't . . . a Luxury:** Whatever you do or don't think of safety, it's not something you can ignore any longer. Your job, your family, our world is simply too precious to be careless with once you know the risks associated with ignoring safety.

2. **Safety Isn't . . . a Waste of Time:** Time is precious. Trust me, no one knows that truism better than I do. But if you're shortchanging safety for other things, thinking that protocol and directions are for other people, the only time you're shortchanging is your own.

3. **Safety Isn't . . . Guaranteed:** I would like to think that my boss, the company who made my ladder, or the other drivers cruising past me on the freeway will all be looking out for my safety, 24-7, but the fact is they are as accident-prone as the rest of us. There is no way to guarantee safety, only practice it every day.

4. **Safety Isn't . . . Just Your Job:** The good news is that the more we care about safety, the more our family,

our friends, our neighbors, our coworkers, and yes, even our bosses will as well!

5. **Safety Isn't... Scientific:** Accidents happen. There is no way to control the uncontrollable, but there is every way to control the pieces of the safety puzzle that are our responsibility. Even if we can't avoid a traffic accident caused by somebody else, we can control things like whether or not we're wearing a seat belt, if we're going too fast to slow down in time, if the kids are buckled up, and so on. It's a dangerous world, no doubt, but that doesn't mean we can give up and be part of the problem. It's on us to be part of the solution, if only for our family's sake.

6. **Safety Isn't... Expected:** One of the saddest things about safety is that it is no longer expected. Our kids flaunt safety at every opportunity and proudly post videos of themselves doing daredevil stunts for the world to see. (Come to think of it, we adults aren't all that shy about our daredevil antics, either.) I recognize a lot of this as the same attitude I had before my accident. I'm young—or not so young—I'm invincible, and it will never, ever happen to me. Of course, now I know different.

7. **Safety Isn't... Mandatory:** Unfortunately, it's not a crime to be a total clown when it comes to safety.

You can generally be as reckless as you want to be, and no one can do a damn thing about it. As long as you wear your seat belt back from the hardware store, of course you can be free to grind, saw, hammer, screw, yank, rip, and tear your way through your days without a single nod to safety or equipment to shield your eyes, hands, or face.

8. **Safety Isn't…Sexy:** One thing safety is definitely *not* is sexy. No one wants to talk about safety, let alone think about it. It doesn't make for good magazine covers or blockbuster movies, but that's the problem—the more we ignore it, the more dangerous our world becomes. It's up to you to make safety "sexy" for you and your family.

9. **Safety Isn't…Macho:** A decade ago if you had seen me at one of the Exxon safety meetings we had regularly—too regularly, if you ask me—you would have probably been like everyone else and steered clear of me. I let everyone know that safety was the furthest thing from my mind, and those who dared wake me as I slept behind my sunglasses soon knew not to make that same mistake again. Chances are, you know someone just like me at your plant, maybe even in your own family—that guy or gal who is so antisafety that they'll go above and beyond to ride anyone who dares put on a pair of safety glasses or dares to wear gloves while han-

dling a lawn mower. But what's more macho? Playing it safe and going home to your kids at night or screaming your way through daily therapy to survive a careless workplace or home accident?

10. **Safety Isn't...Going Anywhere:** Our world grows more hectic, careless, and violent every day. The bad news is that complacency sets in. The good news is that, with this book, you'll finally have the tools you need to treat safety with respect and have practical ways to make sure everybody in your family gets home safe and sound every night.

Parting Words about Safety

At the end of the day, I know that safety isn't the sexiest topic in the world. But having literally walked through fire, I can tell you that there is no substitute for safety. If you are reading this book, you either work in a job where safety is an issue or want to enjoy your family for the longest time possible—or both.

That means neither you nor I can ignore safety any longer.

CHAPTER 7

Safety, It's Everyone's Responsibility

Those who have heard my story, either in person or on one of my videos, are deeply moved by it. I've had audience members come up to me with tears in their eyes—and some of these are union guys right out of central casting—because they were so touched by my story and my message. And that message is powerful yet so simple: **take responsibility.**

That's it. If I had taken responsibility for my own actions that night, I would have worn safety goggles and not damaged the vision in one of my eyes. If I had simply paused, taken stock of the situation, and then spent those ten extra minutes following procedures, I wouldn't be writing this book. And that's my message to you: safety procedures are in place for your benefit, and no one's going to do them for you.

You don't have to be a Teamster suiting up in fireproof clothing and heavy gloves to heed that warning. You can be a guy getting ready to hang some Christmas bulbs on a ladder that clearly says, "Do not step on the top step," and...step on it anyway.

You can live in a 3,000-square-foot house with central heating, two ovens, dozens of blow-dryers, curling irons, and regular irons and not have a single fire extinguisher on the premises.

Whatever we are or aren't—electrician, housewife, CEO, janitor, cop, fireman, nurse, ER surgeon, gardener—we all have a job to do, and that's to get home to our family safe every night.

That's the most important job; that's your only job.

And only you can do it right.

The BS Society

We are a country at war. We're at war with ourselves, with our enemies, with our old way of life, with the new way of life that awaits, with our old ways of doing things and new ways that may not work. In many ways, we're at war with the world.

The attacks on 9/11 and the events that followed were a kind of warning shot that "Hey, guys, maybe the rest of the world isn't as enamored with our way of life as we thought." But what I see as I travel around the country is that, in fact, most of the world wants what we've got.

Workers in China, in Mexico, and in other countries are scrambling to get what we have, and they're achieving it. I was giving a speech at a factory in Malaysia recently, and as I looked out over the audience, I was struck by the difference between foreign workers and our own.

Have you ever seen *Rocky III*? You know, the one with Mr. T? Well, these foreign factory workers had "the eye of the tiger." They were hungry; hungry for our jobs, our cars, our houses, and our way of life. I say that not to disparage any one country or to raise the alarm bell that we should close our borders.

I say that to make this point: we could stand to get a little "eye of the tiger" back ourselves. When I travel abroad I'm frequently told that American workers are lazy. I always laugh. I spend most weeks in gritty, hardworking, massively active plants and factories bursting with energy and productivity.

Are American workers lazy? Hell no. However, when it comes to safety, we *have* become complacent. Maybe not always about policy and procedures, but definitely about personal responsibility.

In fact, I like to say that Americans live in a BS society. In other words, Blame and Sue. When something happens, our first two immediate thoughts are

1. Who can we blame for this?
2. Who can we sue for this?

The direction we look for solutions, now more than ever, is outward, not inward. Rather than accepting responsibility for our own mistakes, let alone being responsible enough not to make the mistakes in the first place, we go about our lives like so much human driftwood, letting things happen to us rather than making our own life happen.

Why do we find it so important to blame others for the life events that we have the power to prevent and avoid? That's right. We can actively prevent 99.9 percent of the accidents, drama, pain, and abuse that happen to us.

Safety Isn't the Other Guy's Responsibility— It's Yours

Take personal responsibility for your own well-being and that of the people around you.

If you see your friend getting into his car after a few too many drinks, stop him. Don't let the awkwardness or embarrassment of the moment—or fear that your friend will be insulted—stop you.

I'll be the first one to tell you that a few awkward—or in the case of safety gear or suiting up, uncomfortable— moments are well worth the peace of mind that comes from saving someone's life, especially your own.

It is so simple, yet I see so many examples of people just avoiding an uncomfortable situation. I see people refusing to be responsible for themselves—and I was one of them for a very long time. I learned the hard way that arrogance or laziness doesn't bring you home at night.

I want people to read this book and really hear my story—in an instant, what should have been years being a father, husband, and son was replaced with years of pain. I spent years in hospitals recovering and having one operation after another. And even more years of therapy—physical and behavioral—that showed me what was truly important in life.

Worse than my own pain was that of my daughters; they suffered terribly as a direct result of my accident. There were terrible repercussions that lasted for nearly a decade after the accident. And why? Because I was too thickheaded to follow simple procedures, and my buddies were too macho to call me on it.

And it happens every day in all sorts of situations.

Mine is an extraordinary story; a spectacularly dramatic event that took away years from my life—but restored me as well. I think you'll find the story unforgettable, and hopefully you'll walk away from this book knowing that you have the power to keep yourself and those around you from becoming another statistic.

As I speak around the country, as I meet people just like you face-to-face nearly every single week, I know it's not just me they're coming to see. People everywhere want to be reminded of just why it's so important to be safe in these trying times.

There's a saying that people are defined by a single moment. I would respond, "Don't let that moment happen." And it can happen in a second. Let's be sure everyone gets to go home tonight, because as I always say, "Everyone deserves a future."

The Blame Game Is for Suckers

As I go around the country speaking to companies, to civic groups, to family organizations, and to everyday people on the street, what I find quite often is that for people to take safety seriously, they often have to get hit by a Mack truck!

Me? I had to get blown to kingdom come to take safety seriously. I hope it doesn't take that for you. I hope that this book, in fact, can be your Mack truck, your own personal kingdom come, your wake-up call for what safety really means—for you and your family.

We've already talked about safety in its literal sense. What does it mean to me? To you? What it is, and what it isn't. So that's basically covering the "what" of the safety equation. But now we get to another all-important question: the "who" of safety.

In other words, **who is responsible for your safety?** On or off the job, at work or at home, in private or out in public, who is responsible for keeping you safe?

Is it...

- the plant manager at work?
- the restaurant where you're having dinner?
- the manufacturer of your child's high chair?
- the movie theater where you're sitting?
- the company that made the seat belt in your car?
- the CEO of your job?
- the other guy?

The fact is, the answer is…all of the above. But that doesn't tell the whole story. There's still one critical factor missing from that equation, and it's **you**. Beginning, middle, and end, safety is up to you. It's also up to me and the other guy and the CEO and everybody on that list.

Trust me, safety will never prevail if we're not all on the same page. Too often, however, we're not even reading the same playbook! Accidents happen when only one half of the equation is concerned with safety. For weeks, for months, for entire years, I blamed everyone at Exxon for my accident.

If management had only replaced those manifolds, if only the blanks weren't so heavy, if only the guys back in the control room had decreased the fuel flow that night, if only the jerk who was supposed to work the shift hadn't called in, if only I hadn't been working that double, if only…

Of course, there was some truth to all of that. But factor all of those variables in, and I would still have been perfectly safe—and none of this would have ever happened— if I'd only followed procedures that night.

Sure, management should have replaced those manifolds years ago, but instead they had put a perfectly safe procedure in place until they did. Sure enough, if that guy hadn't called in, I wouldn't have been working his shift, but I was the one who wanted the extra cash for my vacation and wasn't concerned about sleeping it off on the beach the next day.

I could continue to blame everyone else for what happened *to* me that night, and the answer always came back:

"But it would have been fine if only I had done this...or if I had done that..." It took me years—a lot of long, dark years—before I finally realized that I could only blame myself for the accident.

And what's more, Exxon and the guys on my shift and everyone who had to clean up behind me could have blamed me for my accident! Millions in damages and delays and downtime and lost profits, all thanks to me. And here's the twist: all those years I spent blaming them, no one ever blamed me. Not one person, in all that time of me blaming everyone but myself, ever said to me, "You know, Charlie, you really screwed things up for a whole lot of people that night..."

Not once, not ever.

In fact, the managers and supervisors I had spent years cursing and trashing behind their backs were the very people who helped me and my family not just immediately after the accident, but for years to come.

A lot of what happened to my family while I was in the hospital, the burn unit, or later in rehab was lost on me. I just wasn't around for it, nor was I up to it, physically or emotionally. I either wasn't conscious when it was happening or was too focused on my own survival and, later, drugs, booze, and rehab to give it—or them—much thought.

In many ways, it was less like losing a chunk of your life and more like putting it on hold. The problems of the world didn't so much go away as they simply retreated into the shadows, lurking and waiting to pounce on me the minute

I was released from the hospital—as if God had pushed a big, giant pause button on the remote control called my life.

Of course, it never felt that way for my family. They had school to go to, homework to do, jobs to toil through, and on top of all that, a sick dad who needed visiting at night and on the weekends. While I was focused solely on one type of survival, my family was focused on surviving as well. There was no pause button for them.

There were whole years there where I didn't have to do the basics of adult, human life, such as...pay a bill, cash a check, click a seat belt, lock a door, cook a meal, find a babysitter, enforce a curfew, pick up milk or eggs on the way home, or schedule a simple dental appointment.

Who did all that? The fact is, Exxon took on a lot of that responsibility for me and my family during some of our darkest, bleakest days. The man Exxon sent to talk to my family in the hospital that very first night of the accident was the operations manager at the refinery, Jim Corbett.

Jim was there to explain what had happened and what would come next, where I was and where I'd be going, and for how long and why, and what to expect. Even I didn't know all that stuff, but Jim did. He helped my family understand the difference between this hospital and that, explained what a step-down unit was, and described how rehab worked.

A full year later, as I languished in rehab, Jim was still calling my family, asking if there was anything he could do to help. When my family couldn't find a ride to this hospital or that rehab facility, Jim was there to arrange transportation for them. When my kids needed a babysitter, Jim took care of it. This wasn't a working vacation for him, either. There was no pause button Jim got to push. He did all this on his own time, in addition to his significant responsibilities as plant manager.

The crazy thing was, for the longest time, I considered Jim and guys just like him "the enemy."

There Is No Us; There Is No Them

It's impossible to fully understand the work conditions at my refinery without remembering where I'm from—New Jersey—and the pretty grim relations between management and the union. Now, I was a Teamster all my life; all the guys I worked with were. It's just what you did. And in Jersey, as in a lot of places, the working climate between the union and management wasn't good. We were the good guys, in our eyes, and they were the enemy. That's just how it was, how it had always been for as long as I could remember.

But what I learned after the accident was that there were no good guys and there were no bad guys. There were no "us" and no "them." There were only people doing a job, working to bring home a paycheck—just like me.

For thirty years at Exxon, I was one of "us," not "them." "Us" was a line guy, a blue-collar, working man. "Them" was the suits, the management, the supervisors, and the advisory board.

For many years, hell, for all those years, they were the

enemy. Guys like Jim and his fellow supervisors, they were the bad guys, plain and simple. If conditions were bad at the refinery, it was their fault. If I got stuck pulling a double, it was their fault.

Hammer blanks are heavy and rusty? It was their fault.

Safety procedures too long and complicated? It was their fault.

Safety equipment big and bulky and hot and uncomfortable? Well, that was pretty much all management's doing, right?

Hot, muggy summer night and I had to work? Hell, they probably caused the bad weather!

Forget guys like me running around, leaving trucks on and our safety goggles in the glove box. In my opinion it was management's fault that there were a dozen first aid injuries last month or fourteen reported line accidents last quarter.

The fact is, safety is everybody's responsibility. Yet to many people, accepting responsibility means making sure the other guy is doing his job while we sit back and mark time and hurry up and wait. We can't expect others to keep us safe; we have to take part in our own livelihoods, our own well-being, and ultimately, our own safety.

What's more, we have to look out for—and pick up the slack for—folks who aren't being safe, like me. Sure, it's unfair. No, it's not right. That's why knowing better helps us do better, and now you and I both know better.

Now, you know that if you see a guy without a hard hat on, that could ricochet back on your own safety, so you better warn him to put it on but quick. Guys were always on me about not wearing my goggles or never putting my hard hat on or leaving my gloves in the glove box or whatnot. Now I know why: they were concerned for their own safety.

Think about how many people I endangered by blowing my own self up that night. What if the fire had made it to the main refinery tanks? What if one of the EMTs who fought a fully engulfing blaze to rescue me had lost his or her life in the battle?

No man or woman is an island unto him- or herself, and that's ultimately what safety comes down to: **taking care of each other.** On the job or off, we're all in this together. And I'm not just talking about the guys you work with—or for. I'm talking about your spouse, your kids, your parents, your neighbors, your friends.

So if you can't be safe for yourself, be safe for them. Ultimately, they're part of your safety team as well.

Teamwork: It's a Two-Way Street

After nearly every talk I give, one of the first things people ask me is, "Charlie, what can we do to increase the safety of our plant?" Or... our office? Or our grocery store? Or our warehouse? Or even just our home?

I am fortunate enough to have literally traveled most of the globe speaking about safety to every conceivable type of professional organization. From hazardous jobs—and trust me, they're all hazardous in some way or another—to office jobs, to work-at-home organizations, to hardware stores, I can tell within five minutes of walking onto a site whether it's safe or not.

Safety isn't in the scaffolding or the puddles or the leaks or the posters in the breakroom or the brochures in the front office or the rusty pipes or creaky manifolds. Safety starts and ends with people, folks like you and me. The only safe facilities are those where the people—from the corner offices down to the janitor—work together toward one common goal: safety.

You can't say "Safety is number one" in a meeting and then expect guys to work five double shifts in a row. That's not about safety, that's about the bottom line. And folks can easily read between the lines.

Let's face it: none of us is stupid. We do what we're told, but we also know the score. If you're the top dog at your company and you're just talking safety but not walking it, that message is going to filter down from your office to management to the line to behind the line and then echo back to you in more accidents, not fewer.

It comes down to what works. All those years I had spent cursing and blaming and alienating management, that obviously didn't work—not for me and not for my plant.

Blaming guys like Jim and his colleagues and my other supervisors and ignoring their advice or suggestions as just more corporate speak didn't work. Ignoring procedures and protocol in favor of comfort and looking macho didn't work.

The only thing that did work, for safety or anything else to succeed, was to sit down together at a table—"us" and "them" together at the same time—with a little bit of dignity and respect and to openly discuss, back and forth, what we were going to do as a team to solve this particular problem.

You and me, one problem at a time, finding solutions together—that's what works. Too often safety is about the big picture when what really needs to happen to make a site truly safe is to solve one little problem at a time. But we can't do that when we're so full of blame and finger-pointing that none of us can even agree on which problem to start solving in the first place.

The problem with that whole "us versus them" mentality is that it clouds the real issue of getting down to solving **one problem at a time**. Saying, "Management's to blame for everything," is simply a way of saying, "I'd rather blame someone else than follow this procedure management's put in place to fix this one issue."

But if the procedure is too big and bulky, then fix it. If the procedure's just plain wrong and pigheaded any way you look at it, voice your concerns. You're as much to blame as your supervisors if you don't point out what's wrong and suggest a way to fix it.

It may have been years since your manager was out there in the field, dealing with what you're most concerned about safety wise. If he can't even see the line from his office, how's he going to know what the real day-to-day safety issues are if nobody tells him?

Sit down with management and discuss it. Talk to them like people, make them see your side, and then listen to their side. Maybe you can't do away with that procedure altogether, maybe it's not in the budget to replace the manifolds, but what can you do to compromise?

You Can Build a Brick Wall or Build a Team

Years ago when I was first starting out at Exxon, I overheard a heated conversation on the plant floor. Some boss type needed a job done and was trying to buttonhole some poor plant worker into doing it. The boss shouted at his employee, "I've got a hot job, and I need it done."

The worker took one look at what the supervisor was asking him to do and said, "I'm not doing that job; it's unsafe."

The supervisor immediately got into his brick-wall pose—legs planted firmly apart, arms folded tightly across his chest, chin up—and said, "You're going to do that job."

And the worker got into the exact identical brick-wall pose and said, "I'm not doing that job; it's unsafe."

As for me, I checked out after a few verbal volleys. Now, that was more than twenty years ago, and as far as I know, those two are still fighting to this day, and the job still hasn't gotten done. Looking back, both guys were right. The supervisor needs a job done, and the worker wants it done safely.

I've been on both sides of that fence, and I know the hidden variable in this discussion is the customer who's waiting on the other end of that order, waiting for his shipment of fuel or tennis rackets or sneakers or plastic barrels or nuts or bolts or widgets. For both sides, the argument is very basic: they both want to keep their jobs. But how can they if neither one actually does his job?

So what do you do in a situation like that? Well, when I managed safety for Exxon after my accident, I frequently ran into this kind of brick wall confrontation. Since I represented the Teamsters in this case but wanted to ensure that my Teamsters kept their jobs, I would go to my guys and say, "Listen, guys, you're the experts here. You know this job in and out. I recognize it's not safe, but the job still needs to get done. So how about instead of telling your supervisors you can't or won't do the job, you say something different to them instead? How about you say to them, 'I can't do the job this way, but I can do it that way'? You're the experts, after all. And this way the job would get done and done effectively…"

It was hard to get them to wrap their heads around that one but easy for them to see the logic of (a) keeping their jobs and (b) getting another irate supervisor off their backs!

What's more, the next time that supervisor came to one of them with a hot job he might do it a little differently as well. Rather than approach one of my guys with demand and damnation, he'd seek their advice on the best way to do the job efficiently and safely. And after a couple such interactions like this, both supervisors and Teamsters would magically discover…they're on the same side!

Woods the Toy Maker Didn't Have to Die

The thing not a lot of leaders understand is that teams aren't just collective, faceless, nameless groups; they're made up of individual people with personalities, fears, anxieties, and insecurities. What's more, these individuals relate to each other in specific and unique ways.

Just lumping a group of guys together on a job doesn't make them a team; it's the relationships they form that determine whether or not a team will work well together.

And even if they work well together, if a supervisor doesn't foster an open atmosphere of transparent communication and sharing, well, the team isn't worth much more than the sum of its parts.

Woods was a neighborhood guy, tough as nails but with a sensitive side. He wasn't just good with his hands, he was great. Everyone called him Woods because he was a woodworker. He had a real gift, a real talent. He used to make toys for the neighborhood kids: horses or other wild animals or cowboys and Indians. They were beautiful creations the kids would treasure for years.

But like many artists, Woods needed a day job to pay the bills. Woods liked to say he was an artist by nature and a construction worker by trade. One day on the job, Woods was on the tenth floor of a new building when he found himself needing a wrench to secure a bolt.

So as construction workers will do, he called down a few floors to ask his buddy for a wrench. Now, standing next to Woods was one of his best friends, and he wanted to tell

Woods to put on a safety harness. He could almost see how it would go: Woods reaching for the wrench, missing it, and falling to his death. But despite the premonition, he said nothing. He later said he didn't want Woods, the toughest of tough guys, to think he was a wimp.

And so it happened, almost as the friend had predicted: the buddy down below tossed up the wrench; Woods reached for it, fumbled, lost his footing, and fell ten stories to his death.

At his funeral a few days later, his construction buddies all gathered around the coffin, crying. Tough guys until the end, they found out the hard way that death was even tougher. But they didn't have to find out that way; they didn't have to be there that day, crying.

If just one of them would have told Woods to wear his safety harness, if just one of them would have broken that macho work-site code and been a real friend rather than just another tough guy in a tool belt, Woods would still be alive and handing out toys to neighborhood kids.

It doesn't have to be this way. Teamwork is the art of bringing diverse, often tough people together and helping them work together. Part of working together is looking out for one another. It's a part of teamwork that too often becomes less of a priority than safety itself.

Seven Ways to Foster Teamwork at Work—and at Home

Teams just don't spring up fully formed on the site; they are made by people just like you and me. And what you need to establish at a successful, safe workplace is a strong, unified team that's focused on one thing and one thing only—safety.

With teamwork, you really can accomplish anything. One person railing on and on about unsafe conditions at your plant isn't going to win that person any favors *or* get the plant any closer to a safe working environment.

But when everybody knows what's at risk, when the channels of communication are open and everyone is working toward the same common goal—which is a prerequisite for safety of any kind at any site—then things actually get done.

And that's how safety works: one problem getting fixed at a time. If you can pinpoint, say, six specific safety issues at your workplace and then set about prioritizing them one at a time, you are on your way to fixing all six problems eventually.

And it won't happen overnight, believe me. I often am invited back to speak at plants where safety is an issue year after year. Sometimes it takes several years before the plant is considered safe, but at least they're on the right track. Think what might happen if they never got started in the first place?

You can't imagine the sweeping and plant-wide changes

that resulted in *my* plant after *my* accident. I mean, we're talking a top-to-bottom overhaul of every system, in every department, to see that no one ever became a walking inferno again.

But look what it takes to start those changes! Don't let it come to that. Start working together right now—don't even wait until you finish reading this book to start—so that you and everyone involved can work as a team to enact change ASAP.

Here are seven ways to do just that:

1. **Communicate:** It all starts with talking. If I hadn't sat in so many of those safety meetings, sunglasses on, with eyes and ears closed, I might have said something sooner about my own concerns with the plant safety. But I never did. Start talking now, not later. You've got a chain of command at work, or even at home; start using it. Report directly to your supervisor and express your concerns. If he or she doesn't take you seriously, who's next in your chain of command? Go talk to them. Talk until you'll find someone who'll listen, and then make sure they talk to someone who will listen. That's how communication works.

2. **Listen:** We often think of communicating as merely talking better, but in fact we all need to listen better as well. As you begin to more openly and honestly—and hopefully, respectfully—share

your concerns with coworkers, supervisors, and management, listen to what they're saying. Don't just hear the words *no*, or *later* or *maybe* or *not now* and take it as a refusal, but listen, instead, to how those words are being used. "No" doesn't always mean "no," even if it sounds that way at first. Listen to what folks are really saying and not just what you expect to hear.

3. **Schedule:** You have to make time to take time. In other words, you can talk all day, but until you set something up formally in order to work together as a team, those words will likely be little more than hot air. It's not always easy to foster teamwork in a workplace where multiple shifts are all working on different schedules, but that's why scheduling is so necessary. Much as you would schedule a safety meeting where nothing gets done, you must schedule a meeting about safety to ensure that something gets done. Scheduling might seem insignificant, but it's often the first step in pinning folks down on what exactly their commitment level is to safety. So if your supervisors talk a good game about safety but can't commit to meeting with you to discuss your concerns, keep working until you can get them to commit to sitting down with you at least once. Once they see you're there to discuss issues seriously, further meetings can then be arranged more easily and cooperatively.

4. **Act:** Words and protocols and e-mails and plans are useless if they're just on paper. You have to act for them to have any meaning, let alone power. If there's a safety procedure in place, follow it. If there are steps to being safe, don't skip any. I know it takes longer, I know it may be uncomfortable, I know you have places to go and people to see, but...remember that safety is about making it home safe every night. You can't do that when you're acting rashly and ignoring safety.

5. **Agree:** We've already seen how important compromise can be. I like to tell the groups I speak to that "teamwork is compromise with feet!" In other words, teamwork is compromise in action. It's you and your team doing significant, actionable "stuff" to make safety happen. But first you have to agree with your team on what exactly to do. This often means making concessions, being patient, prioritizing which concerns are most important, and acting on one at a time.

6. **Do Your Part:** All workplaces want to be safe; every home needs to be safe. No one wants to get hurt or burned or punctured or bloodied or blinded by a workplace accident. And yet there are so many every year simply because everyone expects the other guy to do his part—and theirs! But teamwork is all about everyone assuming equal responsibility for

the group's safety. You can't expect Fred to do half your work and Mary Sue the other. All three of you have to do the work equally to pull this off. That's what teamwork—true teamwork—is all about.

7. **Make It Stick:** Finally, you have to commit to whatever the team agrees upon and make it happen, make it stick. I've seen so many teams fall apart simply because there was never a common bond to join them in the first place. If you come together as a team over safety, make sure that you stay together in order to make safety stick. It could mean having more meetings and compromising more often, but it's worth it in the end, because when safety is a team effort everybody wins.

Parting Words about Being Responsible for Your Own Safety: It Only Takes a Moment to Express Your Concern

Part of the unwritten rule on most job sites is that you "go along to get along." I know as I write this, some of you are shaking your heads at the above advice because, frankly, on your sites—maybe even in your own homes—you know the boss doesn't want to hear that his or her workplace might not be the safest one around. He probably doesn't want to add more work to his already overloaded schedule by starting weekly team safety meetings, either.

You may know that your manager is looking for any reason to sack or harass you, or you don't want to risk losing a good shift or your coming vacation days over something as trivial as a leaky gasket, a sticky valve, or a wonky electrical outlet.

But take it from me, the same folks who might intimidate or harass you into keeping your silence will be the first to praise you if you can bring to their attention a safety hazard that could get them in trouble with OSHA (Occupational Safety and Health Administration)—or worse.

What's more, lives are at risk. Yours, theirs, and everyone's is at risk in an unsafe work environment. I'm never in favor of crying wolf if it's just the cat next door meowing on your doorstep, but if there's a wolf clawing at the window, cry wolf!

In other words, safety is everybody's responsibility—starting with your own. Ignoring workplace safety is like not reporting the drunk driver who just clipped your rear end as he roared into downtown traffic. You're putting your life and everybody else who works on site at risk.

What are the procedures for reporting safety hazards at work? Do you know? If so, use them. If not, find out what they are, and...then use them. Tell someone.

It's not just the right thing to do, it's the safe thing to do.

At this point in the book I'm going to start talking specifically about three areas that mean the most to me, and to you, when it comes to your personal and professional safety:

1. Safety at Home
2. Safety on the Road
3. Safety at Work

At home or at work, on the road or on the job, the safer we are, the safer we'll be when we get back to work or when we come back home. Safety is safety whether you're riding a lawn mower barefoot at home, refusing to click your seat belt, or leaving your safety goggles on the dashboard of your truck at work.

CHAPTER 8

Safety at Home

L ike a lot of home hobbyists, Phil liked to build model
boats and airplanes in his spacious basement. A proud
veteran of World War II, he preferred building military
planes and warships. He was proud of them, and they lined
the shelves of his den upstairs.

Like a lot of hobbyists, Phil felt safety was for the other
guy. After all, he worked at home, not at some big plant
with bulky machinery and firing pistons and hazard warnings all over the walls. The radio played his golden oldies,
familiar songs from a bygone era that made him feel safe
and sound in his creaky desk chair.

Besides, Phil worked with sailboats and propellers, paint
and glue, not forklifts and dangerous chemicals. And yet he
worked with a grinding wheel and was supposed to wear
safety goggles just as you would working with a jigsaw or
soldering iron or any other hazardous piece of home machinery.

But as with most safety equipment, the goggles were cumbersome and restricted his vision a little so Phil never wore them. He needed his eyes to get the grinding just right so that his model parts would be perfect.

So when the little hairline crack in the grinding wheel got worse and it finally sheared apart, cracking and flying into a dozen lethal pieces, Phil's eyes were completely unprotected and, unsurprisingly, severely damaged. He wound up blind—not temporarily, but for life.

Phil didn't just make those models for himself. He had a family, a wife and kids, and he'd never see them again. It was hard to blame Phil for what he did or didn't do down in his basement—to him, the safest place on earth.

All I know is that Phil blamed himself for never being able to see his family again, and I don't want you to feel the same way someday simply because you didn't take five seconds to put on your safety goggles, gear, or gloves.

Home: The Safest Place on Earth?

We know about childproofing our homes and fencing in our pools and leashing our dogs and keeping hazardous chemicals where they belong. Then come the holidays, and the lights need to go up on the awning, and nobody's ever around when you need them, so...why don't we just climb up on that ladder and do it ourselves?

So what if the highest point is just out of reach? We'll just climb up on that top step and reach, reach...reach. So what if a sign on the ladder says not to do that? It's a sturdy ladder, you've done it a dozen times before, and if you can just stretch an inch or two higher. Almost there…almost there…and bam, you're another statistic, another victim getting rushed to the ER and about to spend your holiday in the hospital.

If you're lucky, that is.

Then, too, the more elements you add to a home— ceiling fans, tool sets, chimneys, swimming pools, skateboard ramps, fire pits, Christmas lights—the more safety hazards you create for you and your family.

It's easier, it's cheaper, and it's almost always faster to simply do something yourself rather than have someone come out and help you, particularly a trained professional. But…is it safer?

The Second Impact: Leading by Example

I often think about what I taught my kids growing up— about safety on and off the job. I never used to wear my seat belt, ever. Now, of course, I know that when it comes to traffic accidents, it's not the first impact that kills people; it's the second impact.

Now, the first impact is car on car, but the second impact is people on car. And sometimes even people on people. It's what happens when people who don't wear seat belts are thrown out of their seats and bounce around the car, crushing themselves and everything in their path.

If you've ever watched families get into a car, you'll often see the parents turn around and scream at their kids, "We're not going anywhere until you're all buckled in." Then once the kids are safe in their seat belts, the parents turn around and drive off—while not wearing theirs.

If that family gets in an accident, once that second impact hits and the parents go flying around the car, they could end up killing their own children by landing on them, crushing them to death. And I can't imagine anything worse than a parent being directly, or even indirectly, responsible for a child's death.

Even if there is no crash that time or the next time or the time after that, what are we teaching our children when we lead by the wrong example? If I don't wear my seat belt, but I keep telling my kids, "Wear your seat belt," pretty soon once they're able to drive on their own, what do you think is going to matter to them most: what I said or what I did?

What I did, obviously. And so it is at home as well. You can't tell your kids to wear a helmet while going on a bike ride and then not wear one yourself. You can't tell your kids to wear proper safety equipment while using a weed whacker and then not wear such yourself.

What you do is always more important than what you say, and no age group is better at reading between the lines than young children. If you're going to have a safe home, a safe car, a safe site, you have to practice what you preach, and what you preach must be safety first, last, and always.

Get Home, Be Home, Be Safe

No accident is better or worse than another; no tragedy means more or less than the next. But when home accidents are so easily avoided, it still seems somehow more tragic that they occur so often—more often, it would seem, than work-related accidents in really dangerous places.

Maybe it's because some of our work sites are so dangerous that we're also so careful. You walk onto the typical plant floor, and often you just get that dangerous vibe. The first thing you do is start looking for a hard hat and safety goggles.

But home? Home is where the carpet is, the couch, the soft bed and the warm drapes, and the cozy overhead lighting. It's a place where we don't have to act safe because we're already safe. After all, we're home.

I guess home accidents upset me so much because now more than ever there is so much information about home safety out there, you'd almost have to be *not* looking to *not* see it.

Be it on the Web or the back of a can of spray paint or on the box that your new drill bit comes in (in multiple languages and often with pictures just in case), modern companies literally *have* to warn you about the safety hazards of their products.

It's not just because they're nice, it's the law.

It's also a reaction to the pervasive and growing number of household accidents that happen in this country every year, day in, day out. Right about now you probably think

I'm referring to big-ticket item safety issues, like not letting your five-year-old operate the miter saw or using your new putter in a lightning storm. But the fact is, it's not so much the big things that tend to surprise us—we tend to at least pay attention to those—but the little things that do the most damage.

For instance, did you know that according to Electrical Safety Foundation International, "Each year in the U.S., more than 100,000 people are treated in hospital emergency rooms due to a scalding injury"? Or that "[h]ot tap water accounts for nearly 1 in 4 of all scald burns among children and is associated with more deaths and hospitalizations than any other hot liquid burns"?

And it's not just ladders and fire pits you have to worry about. According to Electrical Safety Foundation International, "The most common causes of product-related thermal burn injuries among children ages 14 and under are hair curlers, curling irons, room heaters, ovens/ranges, and irons."

We've all been there, especially if you have young kids or even teenagers in the house. You're minding your own business, set your razor down for five seconds in the morning when the phone rings, and come back to find your five-year-old playing "I want to shave like Daddy does."

Most of the time, the game ends with your kid keeping all ten fingers and toes. But every day for some unlucky family, it doesn't, and it's not worth it when it's so simple to just set your razor down safely out of reach. (Or simply wait until you're done to answer the phone.)

I could go on and on about this stuff, but I'm not really here to walk through each room of your house, making sure your wall outlets are covered and there are childproof caps on every bottle of prescription pills. (You've got a grandmother for that.) What I *am* here to do is make sure that you understand and value the importance of safety for you and your entire family.

That's why I want to spend this chapter talking about something that's very important to me and that I hope your family will embrace as well: the home safety plan.

Five Steps for Creating a Home Safety Plan

A home safety plan is simply a set of guidelines, instructions, reminders, rules, and action steps your family can take to stay more safe more often—in or out of the home. It's a simple, fast, and routine step you can take to protect your family, and once it's done, you merely have to follow it.

You follow safety guidelines at work, right? And if you look closely at them, you'll find that simple steps lead to safe results. You use this machine, and you follow these six steps if you want to do it safely. You're checking this gauge? Well, here are the five things to look for to make sure it doesn't blow up the entire plant.

So why should your house be any different? Your home safety plan is just that: yours. You can cover as much, or as little, as you feel your family needs to be safe.

Do you need to tell your kids where every potentially hazardous chemical is found in the house? Probably not, but it would be a good idea to create a page in your home safety plan with instructions on how to safely store or dispose of such chemicals.

More important than theory is practice:

- Does your family know where the rope ladder is located?
- Do they know how to use it?
- Have they ever seen it before?
- Have YOU?
- Would your spouse or your teenage daughter or your ten-year-old son know how to hook it to the windowsill in an emergency?

This is just one example of a simple solution that can be provided, step by step if necessary, in your very own home safety plan. Again, if you live on the first floor, you don't need a section on rope ladders, but you absolutely need to let kids know where the fire extinguisher is—and how to use it.

The bottom line when it comes to home safety is having a plan and sticking to it. Unfortunately, too few families follow this simple process that takes, on average, about forty-five whole minutes.

STEP 1: INFORM

Start by letting your family know there *will* be a safety plan and that they *will* be following it, period. Again, this doesn't have to be a hardback volume that runs you $400 to print off at the local shop. Nor do you have to spend a lifetime laboring over every word, procedure, or warning.

One great way to inform the whole family at one time without anyone getting mixed messages is to hold one family meeting specifically to talk about your plan, and only your plan.

It's important that no matter how big or small your family may be, everyone knows about the plan and sticks to it. That includes Grandma and Grandpa, your boomerang daughter who came back to live with you at thirty, your teenage son who's never home, and even—maybe especially—the little ones.

Remember, a plan is only as good as the people who know about it, and if you're the only one who knows about it, how helpful will it be if the severe thunderstorm, kitchen fire, or collapsed garage happens while you're not there?

If your family, like many, is hard to corral for one reason or another—school, work, extracurricular activities, boyfriend/girlfriend, sports teams, and so on—here are some simple tips for getting them together as painlessly and as purposefully as possible:

- **National Safety Month:** June is National Safety Month, so that might be the best time to annually update your family safety plan with a family meeting. But create the plan now; don't wait for next June!

- **Schooltime:** Check with your child's teacher(s) to see when and if there is an upcoming lesson on safety. If so, your family meeting could be timed perfectly. If no safety lesson is planned, then ask, "Why not?" and suggest they do so in the near future. Why not? After all, the worst they can say is no.

- **Family night:** Perhaps you and your family get together every week anyway—say, for movie night with a pizza or a Sunday barbecue in the backyard. Combining a family meeting with family night could make it twice as painless and doubly effective.

STEP 2: DISCUSS

At your family meeting, it's important to discuss what safety is, how it works, and how detailed your plan needs to be. Again, this doesn't need to be too elaborate, but just the basics depending on how complex the safety issues are or aren't in your particular home.

For instance, if you live in a small house with not many people in it, your plan is naturally going to be far less complicated than for a large household with lots of people and all their various appliances and added risk that more people imply.

Other factors that affect how complicated your plan needs to be include

- **how many tools there are in the house:** It only stands to reason that if you have a garage full of saws and gadgets and gizmos and tools, the more you're going to have to let folks know how to use them—or at least how to turn them off.

- **how many floors there are:** Getting out of a second or even third story in case of an emergency, or a basement apartment or playroom, can be more complicated than shuffling out the front door of a single-story dwelling. So depending on the size and scope of your home, it can affect your plan.

- **the age of everyone at home:** If you no longer have little kids at home, the plan can be more verbal than visual. For instance, you may not have to spell out every little detail of how to dial 911 on a cell phone or how to unplug the space heater. If you've got older kids still under your roof, the plan can be shorter and sweeter still. The pages of your plan might more resemble notes for a speech, with bullet points such as "Remember Johnny's medication if going to the ER," rather than a step-by-step list of where to find Johnny's medication, what color pill bottle it is, and so on.

- **where you live:** City or country, apartment building or farm. These issues come into play when creating a plan that might, for city dwellers, include helping your family become more familiar with fire escapes and introducing them to the neighbors. For rural homes, your plan might have to include meeting an ambulance or fire truck at the mailbox to guide them to the home. Such concerns need to be addressed individually for each home and/or plan.

Remember, knowledge is power, and the more knowledgeable your family is about safety in your home, the less likely accidents are to happen there. And just as important, the more prepared they'll be when and if they do happen.

I often read stories of three-year-olds dialing 911 or grade school–aged children performing CPR on a parent or sibling and think to myself, *Those are kids who've discussed safety at some point.*

It might have been at school or it might have been at the local fire station during National Safety Month, but just as likely it was while seated around the kitchen table, discussing something very much like our home safety plan.

It's not just kids who need to hear this stuff. You'd be amazed by how quickly, and how wrong, things can go in a happy modern house. Here are some simple scenarios that can turn deadly fast if you don't have a simple, stated plan for dealing with them:

- **Quick, a panful of bacon grease catches on fire.** Do you...know where the fire extinguisher is? Do you have to go more than three rooms to find it? Is it out of date? Out of gas? Do your kids know where to find it? How to use it?

- **Think fast, you fall off a ladder in the backyard while hanging holiday decorations.** Now you can't move. It's a Tuesday morning, and no one else is home. Do you...have your cell phone on you? Scream out for the neighbors? Are they home? When will they be home? What do you do now? And for how long?

- **The local fire department is knocking on your front door.** They say a storm/fire/flood is coming and you have five minutes—not ten, five—to gather your belongings and head to the nearest evacuation center. What do you bring? Are you already packed? Can you be sure you bring everything you need—insulin, cholesterol meds, inhaler, cell phone, cash, and so on—in five minutes or less?

The fact is, just as I used to walk around the refinery playing the part of Cool Charlie, too many families take their own safety too lightly. While it may seem like a nuisance to draw up this family safety plan, one or more of the above examples should make it painfully clear how unprepared most of us are for even the most basic disaster!

STEP 3: AGREE

The best way to create a plan everyone can follow is to make sure you all agree on what goes into it. As you might imagine, this often leads to one lively family debate.

One argument in favor of everyone voting on what goes into the family safety plan is that of ownership. When everyone gets to participate in what goes into the plan, they are more likely to actually use it if push comes to shove.

That's why it's never a good idea to simply create a plan, post it, and try to enforce it all by yourself. Your family should participate in a timely and interactive way that makes the process and the plan real to them. When it's real to them, they'll remember it and, more importantly, remember to act on it in times of trouble.

One way to make the inclusion process easier is to keep a legal pad handy at your family meeting and list all the items you and your family feel should be included in the plan. By discussing each one even briefly, you can quickly keep it or cross it off the list and move on.

Here are some simple tips for making sure the right safety measures are included in your plan:

- **Do a walk-through:** As part of your family meeting or during a second one, go from room to room and invite everyone to spot potential safety risks. From unprotected wall outlets to wobbly ceiling fans to space heaters to the frayed chord of a hair dryer, you can quickly and easily list such danger zones and know to include them in your plan.

- **Take an inventory:** Another way to increase family ownership in the plan and let each family member contribute individually could be to let him or her make an inventory. Everyone can scour the house on his or her own time and, on a blank piece of paper, list the items they feel might warrant a warning, plan, or procedure. Then at a second family meeting—or perhaps even the first if you plan ahead—you can all compare inventories and write up those that appeared on everyone's lists or that certain family members feel most strongly about.

- **Borrow another family's plan:** If someone you know at work has gone through this exercise before, you can ask to borrow their plan and which pieces or parts fit for your own family. Or perhaps your child was asked to do this basic exercise for his class—you could participate in the lesson together.

- **Check online first:** There are a variety of templates for these kinds of family safety plans (some websites call them family disaster plans) online. FEMA, the Federal Emergency Management Agency, offers a variety of resources and template plans online at http://www.ready.gov/make-a-plan.

STEP 4: ORGANIZE

The best family safety plans are **simple to follow, easy to find,** and **quick to use.** That is why I'm always in favor of making them less complicated than more and shorter rather than longer.

You never want to shortchange a plan for brevity's sake, but you also don't want a three-hundred-pound monster your youngest can't even lift, let alone sift through if the backyard shed is on fire!

Carefully organizing your plan can help you make it easier to follow and simpler to use, ensuring that everyone in the family—from the oldest to the youngest—can access it in a minute and begin using it immediately.

Some simple ways to help you organize your plan might be

- **by room:** One popular way of organizing your family safety plan is by room. It's a great way to help your family understand the hidden dangers in every room of the house, from the curling iron and space heater in the master bedroom to the fireplace tools in the living room.

- **by category:** If you want to make your plan easy to use and quick to find, you can organize it by categories such as "natural disasters," "electrical," "cleaning products," and so on. This way, if you're in a panic when one of the kiddies swallows an air freshener pellet because it looks like a piece of candy, you can quickly go to the appropriate section rather than look through the entire plan.

- **by danger/threat level:** You might want to organize your plan according to threat level. This works especially well for families with young children, who might have a hard time distinguishing how a blowtorch is different from a squirt gun! For instance, heavy machinery, space heaters, and even handguns can be considered the highest threat level, which you can either label with a warning color, like red, or a number, like "1." Dangerous chemicals like household cleaners or rat poison could be one level down, followed by prescription medication, wall outlets, and so on.

- **by season:** This one might sound like a stretch, but think about it. In Florida and along the eastern seaboard, hurricane season brings with it a safety plan all its own. Likewise, winter in the north has dangers few in Florida need to worry about, such as space heater fires and other household disasters. Organizing your plan by season might be a simple, quick, and effective way of helping your family know just what to do no matter what time of year it is.

STEP 5: BROADCAST IT

However detailed or simplistic your family safety plan might be, you need to broadcast it throughout your home to ensure that it's in writing, that it's formal, and that it's for real. Again, this doesn't have to be some glossy coffee table book you keep out for company and show your friends.

It can and should be a low-key affair for your family's eyes only, in whatever format—print, electronic, or both—you know your family will respond to. Here are some simple ways to simply, quickly, and affordably broadcast your plan:

- **Print it:** Three-ring binders are a great way to print your family safety plan because they're sturdy, affordable, and easy to update. So if you get some new piece of equipment or a tool like a leaf blower or riding lawn mower, you can easily update the entire plan without starting from scratch.

- **Post it:** Invest in a few low-tech, low-key, low-cost clipboards, and clip your simple family safety plan to each one. You might have one per floor or one

per room or so on. If your plan is a small five-
or six-step matter, you might want to print it up
on your computer, laminate it with a few sheets of
plastic from the office supply store, and post copies
of it in the garage or on the back of the medicine
cabinet door where people can quickly and easily
find it—then use it.

- **Plug it in:** Today's laptops, tablets (like iPads), and
even smartphones can also serve as individual family safety plans that are portable and convenient.
Many such electronic devices have document, text,
or notepad features that can be easily accessed.
Electronic devices also serve as great flashlights in
case the power goes out or a family member is disoriented in the middle of the night. This is not only
a great incentive to keep your family safety plan
short and sweet, but also a great way to ensure that
everyone has one without question.

Parting Words about Safety at Home

By now it should be clear that safety is just as important off
the job as it is on. I know you already knew that, just as you
knew that you needed a family safety plan at some point.

In many ways, as I travel around this globe talking about
safety to tough, hardened guys who look just like me in
those old Exxon safety meetings, I consider it my job, my

challenge, and my calling to simply remind people of the importance of safety.

Again, nobody wants to be unsafe, get hurt, or heaven forbid, put their loved ones in danger. It's just that life happens so fast and things like instruction manuals and warning signs and family safety plans quickly become luxuries rather than necessities.

My hope is that this chapter was a short, gentle reminder of how important family can be and how quickly accidents can happen. We've all been there—that "holy crap" moment where the baby's head just misses the glass top of the coffee table or the ladder wobbles but doesn't tip over or the lightbulb fizzles but doesn't burst, that moment where we think, *Wow, that could have been bad.*

But every day in hundreds of emergency rooms and hospital wards all over the country, it is bad. The difference between a near miss and a tragic accident is often measured in millimeters, not inches, in seconds, not minutes, and the faster we react, the more chances we have to avoid a tragedy.

A family safety plan is the quickest, simplest, and most effective way I know to help protect your family and, what's more, involve every family member in their own protection. With single-parent households and couples working outside of the home with latchkey kids and flex schedules and extracurricular activities, we have fewer people at home less often. Our children grow up faster and are alone longer, and with more technology, we have more stuff lying around the house than ever—lots of it potentially dangerous if put in the wrong hands or even if used wrongly in the right hands.

Many household accidents could be avoided simply by not panicking when and if they do occur. Yet we're so rarely placed in a position of danger that who knows how to react when a grease fire starts or Dad breaks his back falling off the ladder or Junior runs over his own toes trying to start up the lawn mower?

The answer is simple, if not easy: we do better when we know better. And one way to know better is to actively and openly create a family safety plan where the entire family is involved.

Kids, grown-ups, teenagers, and seniors all need to be involved because we're all at risk for those little daily mishaps that could eventually turn into real trouble.

CHAPTER 9

Safety on the Road

It's a tragic thing to watch your children—then grandchildren—from afar and not be able to interact with them as you should; it's even harder to watch your children go through tragedy, even imprisonment, because of a careless accident.

Not too long ago I got a call from a father in a panic. His son had just been arrested for vehicular manslaughter after getting drunk, climbing behind the wheel, and getting into an accident on the way home.

His son's girlfriend in the passenger seat had died, and now he was in jail, facing serious charges and racked with guilt over the senseless loss of life. What's more, his son was crippled—paralyzed from the waist down. Naturally, the father was distraught over the ruination of his son's future.

In many ways, two lives were lost that night: the poor girl, an innocent victim, and a young man facing years in prison for a senseless, avoidable accident that I could relate to all too well.

How many nights had I gotten behind the wheel of a car on the way home from a bar, oftentimes after being cut off by the bartender? How many nights had I wrangled and bamboozled my buddies into letting me drive when we all knew I'd had one too many? What's worse, how many times had I endangered my own family or innocent civilians by driving drunk?

Too many, that's how many.

And even when this man's son got out of jail, or amazingly if he got off, he would still be imprisoned—this time by the wheelchair he'd need for the rest of his life.

What did the father want from me during that frantic late-night call? How could I help him from a thousand miles away? Like everyone else I speak to—in a hospital room, in a burn unit, in rehab, or even in the ER—he didn't want help as much as he wanted...*hope*.

"Tell me everything will be all right, Charlie."

It's a phrase I hear nearly every day, and I'm tired of it—not because I'm heartless or don't want to help, but because in some cases, I'm hopeless. How do you tell a blind man it's okay that he'll never see his grandson grow up? Or a burn victim that his son will grow up and get used to the scars, the wounds, and the father's face he no longer recognizes?

How do you tell a man whose son has killed another human being in a drunk-driving accident that it will all work out in the end? Not for his girlfriend it won't, and not for her family and friends and the loved ones whose lives his son also ruined.

Drinking, Driving...Don't

The Centers for Disease Control, or CDC, estimate that one in three crash deaths involves a drunk driver. How many of us know that one person who's caused a drunk-driving accident? Or worse, who knows one of his or her victims?

Drunk driving is one of the most preventable types of automobile accidents—and indeed, causes of death—on the planet today. I'm not saying, don't drink; I'm saying, don't drink and drive. If you know you're going to drink, if it's your night to celebrate or the party's in your honor—if it's New Year's or your birthday, whatever, great—party on. But figure out how you're getting home first:

- Choose a designated driver.
- Have a backup designated driver.
- Save out twenty bucks for a cab.
- Take a limo/hire a car service.
- Book a room at the venue in advance.

Whatever, however, drink responsibly. And that means don't drive.

Many people see me as a survivor, a success story, an entrepreneur, business owner, or world traveler...even an inspiration. I'm invited to big companies all over the world, flown in on the company's dime, wined and dined and roomed and boarded, and I walk in the conquering hero, there to save everyone's safety problems.

I stand in front of hundreds, thousands of people, and I get the applause and the recognition, and then I go back to my room and there's a message waiting for me; another mother or father, another brother or sister, another boss or coworker telling me of another burn victim or amputee or paraplegic who just needs hope and encouragement and a few words of advice.

And some days, I'm done, I'm busted. I have no advice to give. I have no patience or empathy because I'm fried from the travel and the road and the hopelessness that scars and paralysis and loss of limbs or even life brings. I know the long road they face as a family, as caregivers, as listeners, as hopeless witnesses to the pain and challenges and frustrations of healing.

Every phone call like that just takes me back to the night of my accident and how long it took me to get where I am. I'm still not recovered yet. I know exactly what those families are facing—the sleepless nights, the pain and depression and therapy, both physical and mental—just to get to a point where they can begin to recover.

And I just can't bring myself to tell them that. How could I?

So if I sound angry from time to time, if I sound bitter and hardened, it's because, well…I am. And it's nobody's fault and everybody's fault. It's my fault, it's your fault, it's their fault—we're all to blame because until you're faced with losing it, life isn't always precious to many of us.

And when I go into plant after plant, warehouse after warehouse, production line after production line and see safety at risk, lives at risk, people at risk, I get hot about it.

Because too often people—leadership, management, supervisors—throw big buzzwords like *paradigm shift* and *emotional currency* and others at a problem that is glaringly simple and overly obvious.

Getting Home Is Half the Battle

I consider road safety as kind of a "bridge" between safety at home and safety at work. That's why I wanted to talk about it in the middle of those two critically important topics. Think about it. We spend a lot of time in our cars—driving to work, out to lunch in the middle of the day, driving home from work, running errands here and there, carpooling left and right—to say nothing of folks who actually drive for a living.

"Motor vehicle crashes are the leading cause of death among those age five to thirty-four in the U.S.," according to the CDC. "More than 2.3 million adult drivers and passengers were treated in emergency departments as the result of being injured in motor vehicle crashes in 2009."

This book would be incomplete without addressing the matter of safety on the road.

Seat Belt Safety: If It Can Happen to a Princess, It Can Happen to You

Whenever I talk to a group of people who don't have dangerous jobs, who work in an office, perhaps, or even from home, I'm always concerned. I'm concerned that they'll hear my backstory, listen to a little of what I have to say, and then tune me out, thinking, *Well, thank God, that'll never happen to me! I don't work in a refinery or handle dangerous chemicals.*

I worry about that so much, so I started thinking about what might be the most dangerous accident of our time. It's probably the death of Princess Diana, wouldn't you agree? And I remember, in the wake of Diana's death and the way they kept showing those horrible pictures of the crash site, the first thing everybody did was run around looking for someone to blame.

Actually, that's the first thing everybody does when there's an accident; they look for someone to blame. In Diana's case, the first group they blamed was the paparazzi. Everyone said it was the paparazzi's fault. They were chasing her down, hounding her. Who else could it have been?

Then more news came out, and everyone blamed the chauffeur, who had reportedly been drinking that evening. Other critics claimed there might have been another car, a mystery car, involved that night. I don't know—any or all of those things might be true. I suppose we'll never know.

What we do know, what we can point to definitively, is the fact that the only person who survived that accident was wearing his seat belt. I know it sounds like I'm blaming the victim here, but if Princess Diana had taken responsibility for her own safety and worn her seat belt, she might have survived.

What's even more tragic is that her two sons, Princes William and Harry, might still have a mother. Those are the facts; everything else—the paparazzi, the chauffeur, the mystery car—is hype. Smoke and mirrors.

You've heard me talk about my definition of safety, of how we have to drill down through the hype and the procedures and the drama and the politics and the reporting and the buzzwords to find the real heart of the matter. And the heart of the matter when it comes down to Princess Diana's accident is this: everything boils down to those two boys growing up without their mother.

If she was wearing her seat belt that day, that might not be the case.

If it can happen to a princess, it can happen to you. Lead by example. Teach your kids, teach your family, teach your friends, teach your neighbors, teach your coworkers every time you're in the car with them—every time—to wear a seat belt. It takes less than five seconds to put your seat belt on, and the life you're saving could be your own—and everybody else's in the car.

When Your Accident Really Isn't

What's an accident? Simply put, an accident is defined as "something we can't control." A driver blindsides you in traffic; that's an accident, at least on your part.

You're going along, minding your own business; a guy's brakes go out, and he sails through his red light as you're proceeding through a green; and bam, accident central.

You run a red light, knowing full well the risk you're taking, and blindside someone else? That's not an accident. The cops may report it as such, the guy at the ER might check off "accident" on your file, but you and I both know that was no accident.

Why? Because it was completely and ultimately avoidable. *You* had control, *you* made choices, and *you* caused the accident. That makes it the opposite of an accident.

Likewise, what happened to me was *not* an accident. My very real, very habitual, and yet very controllable behaviors contributed to my accident. I knew the blanks in that junction were old and cranky. I knew the procedure—when performed properly, that is—was time-consuming and costly, and so I chose to ignore procedure and do things my way, the Cool Charlie way. I made a conscious decision and have been paying the price ever since.

So we have to be careful that we don't write behavioral choices off as accidents when, in fact, they can be personally avoided by making better and better-informed decisions.

Are You a Distracted Driver?

According to the CDC, "Each day, more than 15 people are killed and more than 1,200 people are injured in crashes that were reported to involve a distracted driver. Distracted driving is driving while doing another activity that takes your attention away from driving; these activities can increase the chance of a motor vehicle crash."

Now more than ever, with cell phones, texting, GPS, stereos, teen drivers, and dashboards that are more home computer than auto parts, distracted driving seems to be the norm, not the exception.

Are you a distracted driver? Here are a few simple ways to tell:

- **Are near misses more common than parking meters?** If you've ever stopped just short of rear-ending the driver in front of you because of texting, talking on the phone, changing out a CD or radio station, and so on, then **you are a distracted driver.** Now, imagine if instead of nearly running into a car, you didn't catch yourself in time and ran over a person. That's the unfortunate cost of distracted driving in this day and age, and it happens far too often.

- **Do you text while driving?** You should be thrown in jail. You can't text and drive. You can only text *or* drive. It's just that simple.

- **Has your insurance gone up because of your distracted driving?** Bumps and bruises, scrapes and dents, fender benders and dustups, these are all signs of driving while distracted—repeatedly.

- **Do people refuse to drive with you?** If your friends and family won't even drive with you, chances are you're not just a bad driver, but a distracted driver as well.

Distracted driving causes more than just accidents. It changes and in some cases costs lives. Distracted driving can be avoided with a few simple tips:

- **Never text while driving.** Period. End of story. If you're tempted, leave the phone in the backseat.

- **Hands-on driving.** If you must talk on the cell phone while driving, use a headset or the newly designed steering wheels that can be synced with your cell phone.

- **Eye contact.** Keep your eyes on the road. You don't need to see your passengers to talk to them.

- **Listen carefully.** Many drivers are distracted while changing radio stations, leaning over to switch out a CD, or even examining the back of the CD cover.

Pick your station, your CD, or your music before you drive, not during.

Motorcycle Safety: It's Not Just for Drivers Anymore

Mike was a good guy, a family man. He had a wife and two kids, and he worked hard for his family. He was a good provider, and his family lived comfortably—nice house, two-car garage, swimming pool in the backyard, basketball hoop in the front, the whole ball of wax.

Mike's only indulgence was his motorcycle; he loved that thing. And as for many aficionados, the wind in his hair and the breeze in his face were a part of the thrill. He said it was his right to drive his motorcycle without a helmet, and no matter how much his wife argued with him, his kids pleaded with him, or anyone said differently, Mike never listened.

Don't get me wrong; Mike was no Hells Angel. He obeyed the speed limit, signaled properly, knew all the rules and policies and procedures. He was a dutiful driver if ever there was one. But as is the case with so many accidents, it's not you you need to look out for, it's the other drivers.

Then one day Mike went off on a merry ride, obeying the speed limit, looking left, looking right, the wind in his hair. It was blowing beautifully when a drunken driver blew through a stop sign and right into Mike.

Mike's bike was smashed, crumpled into an unrecognizable mass of twisted metal. Mike went flying, landing headfirst on the pavement. His body survived the accident; his brain didn't.

Mike was left brain-dead, permanently. The other driver was uninsured. Mike had okay health insurance, but he wasn't covered for lifelong care. Without his income and needing full-time assistance, Mike's family was left all but destitute. They lost the house, the cars, the pool, the basketball hoop—everything.

They moved into a tiny apartment where the only room big enough for Mike's hospital bed and necessary supplies was the living room. The kids, teenagers now, refused to bring any of their friends over to the house. They loved their father, but for all intents and purposes, their father was gone. What remained was a shell of a man lying in bed wearing diapers.

With no money for professional health care, it fell to Mike's family to care for him. His wife and children had to feed him, bathe him, even change his diapers. And for what?

The fresh air on his face?

The wind in his hair?

Mike's accident, his tragic fate, and the ruination of his entire family was the result of thirty, maybe forty seconds of bad decision making. It would have taken Mike ten to fifteen seconds or less to put on his helmet that day.

And it would have taken that drunken driver another ten to fifteen seconds to hand over his car keys to someone else. Or pick a designated driver—or call a taxi—before going out. Instead, both put their decision-making skills on hold and changed the course of their lives forever.

Mike is far from alone. Per vehicle mile traveled, a motorcyclist's risk of a fatal crash is "thirty-five times greater than a passenger car."

And according to Lawcore.com, "It is estimated that injury or death are the outcome in nearly 80 percent of all motorcycle accidents in the United States. Included in this startling statistic are the nearly 2,000 motorcyclists who die each year as a result of an accident and the staggering 50,000 who are injured in collisions and the like."

Like Mike and his family, tens of thousands of people are affected by motorcycle accidents each year, and it's not always the driver's fault. We can all increase motorcycle safety 100 percent by simply increasing our awareness of how we drive, regardless of whether we're on two wheels or four.

Parting Words about Safety on the Road

Accidents happen every day. That's life. I get that. What I don't get is how we can get behind the wheel of our car (or grab the handlebars of our motorcycle), start up the engine, and then drive off as if we're not launching a two-ton projectile into the most dangerous streets on the planet.

It's complacency, plain and simple. Cars are so technologically advanced, so comfortable, so sleek and dynamic, and what car company doesn't brag about its three-dozen safety features in every commercial?

It's easy to forget we're not actually in our living room as we cruise around the city, texting about our latest plans, updating our Facebook status, or cruising through a yellow light just as it turns red.

Like everything else about safety, it all comes down to awareness:

- **How could we avoid 99 percent of automobile accidents?** Simply being more aware of the road we're on more often. How can we expect others to follow the rules of the road when we don't ourselves? Defensive driving is just that—driving as if the other person doesn't know you're there. These days, you have to drive for two: yourself and the driver next to you. It all starts with awareness.

- **How could we avoid 99 percent of motorcycle accidents?** Simply being more aware that we're sharing the road with them and looking twice before switching lanes.

- **How could we avoid 99 percent of distracted driving?** Put the cell phone down, put both hands on the wheel, and be more aware of the other drivers who don't follow this advice.

Look, you think I like sounding like everybody's grand-
father all the time? Certainly not, but you would, too, if
you'd spent as much time as I have lying in a rehab bed
next to people—young people, old people, men, women,
lumberjacks, housewives, teenagers—who've been in easily avoidable car accidents that have permanently damaged
them. And those are the lucky ones, the ones who've survived.

Don't let it happen to you, to your passengers, to the car
in front of you that you run into—or the pedestrian you
run over—because you're talking or texting on your cell
phone. Because you're distracted, frantic, late, busy, or just
reckless.

I always tell my audiences, "Your car isn't a means of
transportation; it's a flying missile loaded with jet fuel."
When you think of it that way, it's just a little easier to be
safe on the road. To get where you're going and back just a
little more safely.

CHAPTER 10

Safety on the Job

One of the highlights of my job is getting to travel to exotic locations and speaking to new friends and faces about safety. And one of the highlights of highlights was being invited aboard the USS *Nimitz* to speak about safety to the fine men and women of the United States Navy.

Of course, while I was there I was able to knock off more than a few items from my own personal bucket list. Not only was I a few miles off the coast of Afghanistan, but also I got to ride in a jet fighter, geared up and all, being propelled off the deck of a giant aircraft carrier and into the sky—the thrill of a lifetime!

Even more thrilling than the ride along on an active jet fighter, however, were the brave men and women I got to spend time with during my visit.

Frankly, I don't know why they invited me. I think this was one of the first speaking engagements where I learned more from the audience than the audience learned from me.

At night I would go out on deck and watch the fighters disappear into the night, one after the other. Everything ran like clockwork. I mean, I've spoken at some major Fortune 50 companies and seen the best of the best, but this was precision teamwork like nothing I've ever seen before or, frankly, since.

The flight deck was like a ballet. Signals were sent and read, timing was precise, and one after the other those pilots were catapulted into the night sky, off on another dangerous mission to keep country, home, and family safe.

What impressed me most was the courage of these fine men and women aboard the USS *Nimitz*. Not for their obvious bravery flying missions over Afghanistan, where sudden death awaited them in the sky, on the ground, and everywhere in between. No, I'd expected to meet heroes.

The heroism I saw went much deeper than that. What I saw in the quiet conversations, the insistent urging, the playful cajoling, and the occasional blunt reminding were soldiers who cared about each other.

I saw it in the way one pilot would check the guy's parachute in front of him, tightening a strap here or checking a buckle there. I saw it in the way the flight crew went over those jets. They were all looking out for the guy they bunked with, the girls they ate dinner with, the friends they took trips with on leave, and the brothers and sisters in arms who'd signed up for one of life's most dangerous assignments.

Here were the macho of the macho who put me to shame

on my best day. Yet none of them, not a single one of them, was too afraid or sensitive to remind their fellow soldier to buckle up, strap in, get their head in the game, or get out of the plane.

Here I'd found people who cared as much, maybe even more, about safety as I did. I didn't think it was possible. For these brave men and women, life really did hang in the balance. One wrong maneuver, one faulty gauge, one leaky valve, one loose strap or broken buckle could very well mean the difference between life and death.

These soldiers cared about each other and not just because it said to in the manual. But that was no surprise. It was clear that from the way their superiors spoke with them, instructed them, guided them, and taught them, these soldiers had learned by example.

On the *Nimitz*, safety really did come from the top down. It struck me as I said good-bye to my new friends and returned stateside that we could all learn a lot from our brave men and women in service.

No, they're not perfect. They're young and brash and eager and flashy and occasionally loud, but they know more about safety, risk, and danger than most of the plant managers I know. These battle-hardened soldiers, guys and gals who literally flew in the face of danger every night of their young lives, were so concerned about their buddies to check that packs were tight, chutes on properly, and their boots were buttoned.

Yet how many of us get embarrassed or awkward or anxious or downright afraid to tell our spouse to buckle up in front of the kids, or won't take the keys from a friend who's about to make the worst decision of his or her young life and get behind the wheel of his car stinkin' drunk?

Safety will happen when and only when we care enough about our coworkers, our spouses, our friends, our family, and ourselves to say, "Stop what you're doing; it's unsafe. You're going to hurt yourself, you might hurt me, and if you get injured or die, think about what it will do to me and your family…"

I know it's not easy, but it's glaringly obvious and embarrassingly simple just the same. So, how knowledgeable are you about safety? Not just from reading this book, but also in your own life, on your own job, or even in your own home?

Fortunately, there's a quick way to find out.

Test Your Safety IQ

The following Safety IQ Test isn't for credit, and it's not designed to make you feel good or bad. Like any test, it's simply intended to assess your current knowledge level. In this case, it's to gauge your knowledge about one thing and one thing only: **safety.**

Don't be shy, and whatever you do, don't answer in a way you think your boss or supervisor would want you to. Instead, answer these questions openly and honestly; no one will ever read them, so you're the only one who can ever know how you answered. While most of these can be answered with a simple "yes" or "no," there is no right or wrong, pass or fail answer.

This is time for a sincere and honest gut check, not only about how safe your workplace might be, but also about how much you yourself know—and even care—about safety.

QUESTION 1: DOES YOUR WORKPLACE HAVE FORMAL SAFETY GUIDELINES AND...DO YOU KNOW WHAT THEY ARE?

When I ask this question at my presentations, the answer to the first part is almost always "yes," but when it comes to the second part there is generally some grumbling and frequently no easy answer.

Many employees are handed—or at least informed of—the site's safety guidelines their first day of employment and then...never again. Or if never, rarely. Sometimes that's because the plant leadership doesn't make safety a priority and those guidelines are merely a formality. Other times the guidelines are simply understood; you learn them once, practice them often, and soon enough they are a habit.

Having safety guidelines and knowing them are two different things. Again, just as any job requires you to do something well, they also require you to do it safely. While it's ideal to be frequently reminded of safety guidelines, new and old, it's not mandatory, and in fact, plant management might expect you to get them once and use them often.

Whether you know your plant's formal guidelines or not, you probably know how to do your job safely or you wouldn't be reading this! The question becomes, "Does the next guy? Does the new guy?" Only when everyone is on the same page of the safety guidelines is a line truly safe.

QUESTION 2: DO YOU KNOW WHERE THEY ARE/HOW TO FIND THEM IN A HURRY?

Safety guidelines are all but worthless if a company spends five figures to hire a consultant to write them up, another five figures printing them and sending out press releases to say they've printed them, and then promptly puts them on a shelf and files them away.

For one, safety guidelines should be living, breathing things frequently updated and regularly posted. If new equipment is installed and thus new safety protocols put in place, those should go into the old guidelines, and new ones should be printed up and posted and/or distributed.

They should also be readily available and visible for new hires, transfers, workers, supervisors, management, and leadership alike. Everyone should know them and follow them—everyone.

QUESTION 3: WERE YOU PROPERLY ORIENTED ABOUT WORKPLACE SAFETY AS A NEW HIRE?

The best and most opportune time to share a site's position on safety is not only upon a new hire's first day, but also at first glance. In other words, plant safety should be omnipresent even to the new guys sitting in HR waiting for an interview.

I'm always impressed when I go to a work site and see safety posters, signage, and awards outside the warehouse and creeping closer and closer to the front office, even in reception.

These are the plants with year after year of Safest Site in the Region plaques going back as far as one can remember, the plants with those sizable 493 Days without an Accident signs displayed for all to see. I've seen plants with banners on the front door that brag about safety, and that's when I know I'm walking into a plant that cares about safety.

Of course, banners and badges don't always mean safe working conditions, but generally they are evidence of leadership that cares about safety. The sooner HR can spread that message to new hires, the better prepared they can be to come to work, from day one, ready and committed to safety.

If management and their direct reports follow that message up with orientation or safety training specific to that job, and the new hire sees this pro-safety attitude on the floor and in the actions of his or her coworkers, you can bet that he or she will get the message: safety really is number one.

QUESTION 4: WOULD YOU KNOW WHO TO REPORT TO IF YOU HAD A VALID SAFETY COMPLAINT?

Every workplace has a chain of command, but some that have highly hazardous jobs—or simply work with highly hazardous materials—have a safety resource manager. I became one after my accident when Exxon hired me to help manage plant safety overall.

If your site is lucky enough to have one of these resource-ful people, they're likely the clear choice. But what if yours doesn't? Who would you go to then? Your direct report? What if he's a clown who's as interested in plant safety as Fred Flintstone or Homer Simpson?

It's never ideal to break the chain of command—we all know that. Plant politics can be intense, and in some cases if you want to keep your job, it's important to be as diplomatic as you are dogged about safety issues. But if plant safety is at issue, if people's arms and legs and hands and feet and very lives are at stake, there comes a time when even diplomacy must take a backseat to what's right—and above all what's safe.

QUESTION 5: DOES YOUR IMMEDIATE SUPERVISOR TREAT SAFETY AS IF IT'S A NUMBER ONE PRIORITY OR NUMBER TWO?

There is often quite a divide between what is said about safety in the employee breakroom when the big boss is around and what actually happens on the plant floor when it's just you and those humming, spitting machines around.

All that matters, of course, is what happens on the floor. It's likely the CEO won't be there when your ponytail gets caught in the thresher or you open the steam bath five seconds too soon. In the grunt and grind of day-to-day work, it's you and the rest of the line that matters; we all know that.

Even so, the climate on the line is often dictated by your immediate supervisor, and if he treats safety as number one, that's likely how the rest of you will treat it as well. Of course, there's always that Cool Charlie on every site who ignores, even flaunts, those safety concerns, but generally the majority will prevail and keep him in line.

I know that one of the most heartbreaking realizations for me after my accident was how badly I'd let everyone down that night: my coworkers, my direct report, my supervisory team, and the managers who'd been so good to me for so long. To think that I'd put their jobs, if not their lives, at risk nearly broke my heart and drove me crazy.

But you don't have to go through what I did to appreciate safety. I'm telling you now that if it's safety you want, then it's teamwork you need. Everyone needs to be on point—not just you and the guy next to you, but also the guy holding the clipboard at the end of the line and even the guy signing his checks. And if they're not, it's up to you to make sure they are.

Even if all you do is speak up and speak out, you have to do something. Your safety and everybody else's on site is at risk. I don't care if you work at a fast-food joint and the fryer's been acting hinky lately, if nobody's taking your complaints seriously, make them do so.

All it takes is one poor teenager who doesn't know any better to be on the receiving end of a grease fire during his after-school job, and how would you feel then? No job ever in the history of jobs is worth an employee's life—not yours and certainly not mine.

QUESTION 6: WOULD YOU KNOW WHAT TO DO, IMMEDIATELY AND THANKS TO ON-SITE TRAINING, IN CASE OF AN ACCIDENT AT WORK?

The fact is, I knew exactly where to go and what to do in the moments directly after my accident. In fact, I caught on fire directly because I was following procedure, heading for the chemical shower farther down the line.

Unfortunately, by then it was too late. The type of training we need is preventative as well as emergency. In other words, it's better to train a guy how to avoid an accident than it is to teach him where to go if one occurs. Not that you don't need both, but think about it: how often would you need the second if you really trained hard on the first?

Now, everybody thinks that training is just for the new hires—it isn't. In fact, I'll go so far as to say that it's rarely the new guys who cause industrial accidents. Why? Because they've been so thoroughly and recently trained; everything is still fresh in their minds.

What's more, they haven't been untrained by the old-timers yet. But give them a chance! The fact is, workers both new and old need to be trained or, in the case of old-timers, retrained in both accident avoidance and response.

Too often, guys who have been on the job twenty or thirty years do things their way, not the safe way. I should know. I was the original old-timer, grizzled and hard, hungover and bitter. Management was the enemy; the only "friendlies" on site were my coworkers on the front lines.

It was us versus them, and since they'd written the safety manuals, they'd provided us with the procedure, and I was instantly against it. So anyone I trained, I trained in the Charlie way, not the management way.

Once upon a time I was ashamed of that fact. Today, however, I still get to train them in the Charlie way—that being, *don't* do it the Charlie way! And I do believe that I've taught thousands of people how to be safer by showing them what *not* to do, even if I have to hold myself up as the ultimate example.

QUESTION 7: WOULD YOU TRUST YOUR COWORKERS TO KNOW WHAT TO DO ABOUT/WITH YOU IF YOU WERE IN AN ACCIDENT?

The real issue of workplace safety is what others might do in case of an accident. Very few of us work alone, and hopefully, none of us work in a vacuum. That means if we're hurt during a workplace incident, we would have to rely on others for our immediate rescue and recovery.

Like most safety issues, this is a double-edged sword. When an accident happens, the immediate response is an emotional one: "Let me help my brother(s) in arms! I'll risk life and limb to do it. I don't care, just let me in there."

But the time for emotion is gone; now is the time for reasoned, logical, diligent restraint. In the case of a chemical leak, for instance, rushing in to save a fallen comrade can result in an additional death: yours.

Wait and get your safety suit on, and then rush in to help. At least, that's what the old-timers at Exxon taught me once upon a time ago. Again, it all comes down to procedures. Knowing what they are, where to find them in case you've forgotten, or even who to consult/call can save additional injury and perhaps even loss of life.

If you don't know now, find out what to do in case of an accident. If you know and your buddies on the line don't, tell them. We can no longer be afraid of looking silly, wimpy, or less macho when it comes to safety.

QUESTION 8: WHO WOULD YOU SAY IS THE "SAFEST" PERSON YOU KNOW ON SITE?

At Exxon, I worked with a guy named Jerry who was the unofficial safety expert on site. He wasn't management, wasn't a supervisor, but he knew safety inside and out and wasn't afraid to let me—and everybody else—know it.

Jerry always bugged me because I knew he was right and I just didn't want to hear it. I wasn't in a place to hear it. Wasn't Jerry's fault, it was mine, but Jerry was too polite to pry. He just kept on warning me, and I kept on ignoring him.

In later years, after the accident and during my recovery when Exxon had hired me back as safety manager of all things, I became the new Jerry. And just like him, I thought nagging and yelling and cursing and reminding would be enough to get my guys to wear their gear, but I was no more effective than Jerry was.

At least, not until I made safety personal for my guys. So if you have a Jerry on site, and I know you do, train him specifically in how to approach workers in a peer-to-peer setting. If he's management, give him an ally on the line so that they can work together. And whatever you do, don't promote him away from where he's needed most—on the floor.

Take the time to nurture guys like Jerry, and train him to be more effective at drilling safety into his men by making it personal for them.

QUESTION 9: WHEN WAS THE LAST TIME YOUR DEPARTMENT DISCUSSED SAFETY?

Yesterday?
  Last week?
  Last month?

Last year?

Can you even remember? Some plants routinely discuss safety and have meetings whether there's a new protocol to discuss or simply to review old protocols that need discussing.

Some sites have regular monthly or even weekly meetings, depending on the threat level on the floor or simply because of the plant's leadership being dedicated to safety. Then again, more meetings don't necessarily mean more safety. They could have had a safety meeting every day at Exxon—and it often seemed like they did!—and it wouldn't have mattered to me until, well, it mattered.

More important than quantity of meetings is the quality of meetings, and more important still is the message you hear while you're there. Sincere safety meetings often mean that leadership sincerely cares about safety.

QUESTION 10: ON A SCALE OF 1 TO 10, WITH 10 BEING THE HIGHEST, WHERE WOULD YOU RATE YOUR SAFETY IQ?

Finally, rate yourself on a scale of 1 to 10 when it comes to safety. In the 1 range, you are about where I was thirty years ago—Cool Charlie who couldn't be bothered. A little further up the scale, you're probably like most American workers, a 4 or maybe a 6 who isn't reckless exactly, but who probably doesn't know the difference between OSHA and IHOP.

The higher you go up the scale, naturally, the safer you are. My goal isn't to help you be a 1 or a 2, a 4 or a 6, or even an 8 or a 9; my goal is for everyone within the sound of my voice or the reach of this book to have a safety IQ of 10, period. End of story.

It doesn't take much—at least, not much more than what most of us do day in, day out at work. After all, having a safety IQ of 10 is what's required for us all to come home every day safe and sound to our families.

It means, quite simply, the following:

- You know the safety procedures at work and follow them.
- You show up to work aware and on task at all times.
- You know that safety is your responsibility.
- You know where to report a safety violation or hazard and let everyone else know as well.
- You try to get the rest of your team/department to have a safety IQ of 10 as well.

There's no way to really score this test other than to take stock of how you felt as you were taking it. Were you shaking your head no to lots of the questions? Maybe even all of them? Did you only know the answers to half of them—or less?

There's no shame at working in an unsafe plant, only risk. If because of this book, you are suddenly the most-informed person about safety on your line, or even on site, then pass this book around. Give it to your coworkers, your boss, your supervisor, whoever you know who will read it and invest in it. Quote from it frequently. I won't mind!

Don't keep safety to yourself. Instead, spread it around. Take the personal approach, rather than play the blame game and point fingers and accuse and abuse.

If you're a supervisor or management, or even a leader or company owner, this material can save lives in your plant, period. You owe it to your people to make the work environment safer one person at a time.

If it helps, pass the safety IQ questions around. Take a formal or informal poll of how people answer. You may be pleasantly surprised or sorely disappointed. Add questions; delete some; personalize the test for your industry, people, or site; and share the results with plant leadership.

Point-blank, involve others. Safety is personal; it's also communal. On the road, we must drive carefully, reasonably, legally, and defensively. That means driving in a vacuum isn't driving safely. We must also be on the lookout for other drivers who might drift into our lane or cut us off or run a red light or otherwise endanger us or our families.

Would you ever dream of gunning it straight into the intersection the minute the traffic light turns green? If you're like most people, you pause for a second or two to make sure some daredevil hasn't just run a red light and is headed straight for you.

It's not fair, it's not right, but it's safe. And you owe yourself and your family that much. Workplace safety is no different. It's human nature for some people to care more about others than the rest. It's called empathy and not everyone comes equipped with it, but we all can learn it.

When you make safety personal, you teach empathy person by person by person. And you create a caring, safe work environment. We can all be defensive drivers just as we can all become defensive employees. That doesn't mean we rebut everything our supervisors say; it means we look out for danger even if we're not responsible for causing it.

It's not just the right thing to do; it's the safe thing as well.

"That's Not My Dad!"

Recently I was in Australia speaking at a big event. After the event one of the plant supervisors asked me to speak to a man who'd also been burned. Of course I said yes, and before I knew it I was standing in another hospital room, this one halfway across the world, speaking to another burn victim whose dressings were oozing and staining the bedsheets.

He'd been burned severely; one of his ears and part of his nose were missing. He was terribly disfigured and would be for life. The plant manager had asked me to give this man and his wife some hope for the future, some words of encouragement.

And that's what I did. I told the man, "It will get better."
I told the wife, "It will get better."
Before I left, the man told me a story. His young son had

come into the room to see his father for the first time after the accident. The kid was five or six years old. He took one look at his father and proclaimed, "That's not my dad!" He quickly ran from the room and hadn't been back since.

I was instantly reminded of my own mother's reaction the first time she'd seen me. She hadn't recognized me, either. How bitterly the words she'd said that day ("That's not my son!") still sting. I did my best that day, talking to that man and his wife, but I'm not sure how much hope I'd offered him.

Next it was on to Ireland, where again I got a call to speak to a brave and sincere man named Ken Woodward. Ken worked for Coca-Cola and had been blinded in an industrial accident.

Ken shared with me the story of how his son had recently had a child. The whole family had gone over to the son's house to see the baby, and as the new mother proudly passed the child around the room, the baby finally landed in Ken's arms.

Ken told me how the entire room had suddenly grown silent as, one by one, they realized what Ken just realized: He would never see that baby's face, never watch his grandson's first steps or see his yearbook photo or watch him graduate college or see what his future bride might look like.

I felt Ken's pain. Though I could see my grandchildren's faces and watch them enjoy their birthday parties and blow out their candles and win sack races with their mothers, my scars make it impossible for me to lift them over my head and onto my shoulders or to even gently place them on a swing set.

Safety: Personal or Priority?

People wonder why I show my scars at every presentation. They ask me afterward if I'm not insecure about my scars or nervous or maybe a little shy. Of course I am. I don't enjoy doing it, but I feel like I have to do it if I want to make my point. These scars are forever. I'm not happy about them, but I'm not ashamed of them, either.

Every person who sees my scars gets a visible reminder, an in-your-face souvenir of what it's like to experience an industrial accident. Every time I show them, I feel like I'm doing my part to save another life, to give another warning, to give a face and a name and a tragedy to the nameless, faceless issue of safety and how most companies treat it.

One of my main goals for writing this book is to increase **your participation** in not just your own safety, but also the safety of your coworkers and the safety at the plant in general.

Yes, I want your boss to get involved and HR and the gals in the office and the guy on the line next to you and everybody on your site as well, but…they're not here right now, you are.

Safety starts and ends with you. The surest way to make a workplace safe is for everybody to get involved, one person at a time. If you do it and I do it and he does it and she does it, then pretty soon...we're all doing it, and we won't need books like this one. (Hey, let's not get carried away here!)

But seriously, if everyone was doing their jobs right now—the simple, safe jobs they were paid to do—I wouldn't be writing these words, and you wouldn't be reading them. The sad truth about life, as you and I know it, is that there are givers and takers.

Are You a Giver or a Taker?

If you've ever been assigned to a group in school, say for a research project or term paper or oral report, you'll know exactly what I mean. You get four kids together, sitting around a table, and sure enough one of them is going to whip out a notebook, sharpen her pencil, and get to work.

She'll outline group roles, set a schedule, create clear weekly goals, assign duties, and by the time she looks up from filling her first page, she can already see the future. There her lab or group or class partners are, texting or passing notes or doodling or doing anything but participating.

She'll do all the giving (the work) and they'll do all the taking (the grade), and by the time the report is due, they'll reap her benefits as if they'd truly participated all along. But she'll do it because she wants that good grade, because she is a giver and wants to succeed. And why shouldn't the others as well?

And that group dynamic will persist until she does something to change it. Really, adults are no different. There are givers and takers in every walk of life. I'll sit in a restaurant and watch one waitress zip around from table to table, pouring coffee, taking away some plates, dropping off others, wiping one table down, setting another.

Doesn't matter if it's her section or not; she's a giver, a team player, and a go-getter. Meanwhile, three other servers will be sitting behind the counter, doing their nails and letting her bus their tables, and generally only stepping foot on the floor if one of their customers needs something. But where do you think the tips go when it's time to collect?

Workplace safety is no different. I know because for years and years, for decades even, I was a taker. Even if safety really was number one at Exxon, and it was, to me it was more like number 101.

Even if everybody else took it seriously or enough of my coworkers did their jobs, the plant was safe enough that I didn't need to do any more than show up, do my job, and hope not to get blown up by the end of the day. (Well, we all know how *that* turned out now, don't we?)

I'd let guys like Phil, my direct report—and a born giver—cover for me, take the heat if I was late or did something sloppily, or simply pick up the slack for me if I couldn't be bothered to fill out a safety report or write up an incident statement. Phil was the industrial equivalent of that one kid who winds up doing all the work for his or her entire group—he gave, we took.

It's human nature. If someone is ready and willing to do twice as much work, well...that means I can get away with doing half as much and the work will still get done because guys like Phil even life out for guys like me. Or at least, the old me.

Unfortunately, there aren't enough guys like Phil on every plant floor. So you've got one Phil for maybe a half dozen slackers, and pretty soon, the balance is off. The problem is, there are way too many Cool Charlies out there and not enough Phils. But I'm trying to do something about that, starting with these words.

Guys like Phil can't keep up with all the incidents, all the hazards, all the leaks and spills and cracks and faults. But if no one else will, how far can my department's Phil, and your department's Phil, be stretched before something, somewhere breaks and an incident happens?

Life would be a lot easier for Phil and his plant and your plant and mine if we all did just a little. That way, Phil wouldn't be responsible for so much. If I wear my safety equipment, then Phil doesn't have to nag me every Monday morning shift and his time can be better spent (a) doing his job and (b) worrying about his own safety.

The more guys who handle their own business, who do the jobs they're paid for on time, well, and without complaint, the safer the plant is, the more productive it is, and the less responsibility any one person has for everyone else's safety.

It's about personal accountability, about being accountable for, being responsible for, your own butt on and off the line. You wear your equipment so nobody has to tell you, "Hey, Charlie, come on. What is this, the fourth time this week I've had to ask you about your goggles? Just do me a favor and put 'em on already..."

How many times did I hear that, week in and week out? And it never quite penetrated. Why? Two simple reasons: I was being a taker, and I couldn't be bothered to be accountable for my own actions. And that, my friends, is a guaranteed recipe for an accident, an incident, for injury, and even death.

This chapter is all about your attitude about safety, about how you can participate more, and finally about how you can make safety not just more of a priority, but how you can make it a personal priority:

Stop Asking "Victim" Questions

The problem with most plants is training. We often get mixed messages from day one on any site. We see safety signs all over the HR Department's walls and get handed this beautiful bound book full of safety procedures; then we tour the site and see cracks and leaks, and inside we're thinking, *This doesn't add up.*

So it starts with the hiring process and the first taste of safety orientation we get on the job. Despite all the signage and every one of those safety procedures and protocols, new hires aren't necessarily trained to ask, "What can I do to make this situation safer?" Instead, as part of procedure company-wide, they're trained to ask everything but.

So when they see an accident, a spill, a violation, or

even an injury, the first and most basic drummed-in instinct of corporate-trained employees is to seek answers outside their own sphere of influence.

In other words, rather than looking inside for the solution, they've been trained to seek outside assistance:

- "Why aren't you wearing your safety goggles?"
- "Don't you know those are the rules around here?"
- "Why did that happen?"
- "Who is responsible for this area/department/ incident?"
- "Why are they doing that?"
- "How did this happen?"
- "Who can I report this to?"
- "Who is going to take care of this?"
- "When are they going to get here?"
- "Why aren't they here yet?"

It's good that the employee's first instinct is to act, but not so good that most of this so-called action is spent waiting around for someone else to solve the problem.

See, these are all what I call "victim" questions. A victim question is something you ask when you're not in charge of your own destiny, when you're a victim of someone else, of time, of circumstances. You're not given the power to act **on your own,** so you wait for someone to act **on your behalf.**

Instead, take charge of your own behavior, your own reactions, and more importantly, your own actions. Many unsafe work sites persist not because leadership purpose-fully wants to run a hazardous site or even because workers blatantly look the other way.

Instead, sites become unsafe—and stay that way—principally because no one wants to say anything, no one knows what to say or who to say it to or even when to say it. It's not quite apathy or indifference that's at fault, but a general attitude of "that's not my department."

Well, maybe not technically, but if you're working in an unsafe plant are you thinking that what, the chemical leak will somehow fly all around the plant but magically avoid you? That you'll be the only one to escape as that crack in the foundation finally sends the roof crashing down? That you're somehow fireproof or bulletproof or accident proof?

The fact is, safety is everyone's department. So instead of asking victim-type "why" and "who" and "when" and "how" and "where" questions, start asking "me, myself, and I" questions such as:

- "What can I do...to get this spill cleaned up?"
- "What can I do...to make sure this is reported im-mediately?"
- "What can I do...to bring attention to this safety hazard?"
- "What can I do...to impact this situation posi-tively?"
- "What can I do...to make a difference?"

Don't Work to Avoid Failure, Work to Find Success

When it comes to safety, most of us simply work to avoid failure. In other words, we do the bare minimum to avoid getting hurt. I definitely worked to avoid failure back when I was Cool Charlie, sitting in on safety meetings with my feet up and my sunglasses down and my brain on autopilot until the meeting was over.

In the rare cases when a quarterly report was due or proficiency needed to be met and we were actually going to be tested on this stuff, I didn't take notes myself. Instead, I'd have a pal take them, and I'd check in on his after the meeting (if I even bothered to do that).

I didn't go to those safety meetings because I wanted to; I went because I had to. I went because they made me. In other words, I went to avoid failure, not achieve success.

I know safety isn't the sexiest subject on the planet. I get that. But just the same, as I can tell you firsthand, it's deadly serious business. When we're talking about failing at safety, in our jobs, in the plants I visit, on the lines I've worked on, we're talking about injury—maybe temporary, maybe permanent—and sometimes even death. We're talking burns and scars and broken bones and twisted limbs and blindness. So when it comes to safety, we can't just work to avoid failure; we must seek to find success.

When Failure Becomes a Habit

The problem with making "avoiding failure" your default setting or attitude about safety on site is that you not only come to expect failure when it happens, but you accept it. Your bar is set so low you're almost doomed to achieve that which you avoid.

So if one of your year-end jobs is to achieve the unenviable and potentially unrealistic task of making your department 90 percent hazard-free and your attitude is to avoid failure, then you'll neither be surprised nor fazed if you only wind up handling 85 percent of the local hazards. And heaven forbid you work harder to make your department 100 percent safe.

And the danger there is that the lower your bar is set—that is, working to avoid failure versus to achieve success—disappointments become your new default setting and apathy starts to set in. You figure, "Well, I only have to get this machine to a 90 percent acceptable degree of safety, and no one's expecting 100 percent, so...what are they gonna do if it's only 85 percent safe? Fire me?"

And when you don't meet your goal and nobody says anything and you still have your job, there's your answer: 100 percent isn't necessary, even 90 percent is too high, and 85 percent is plenty good enough. So failure isn't just a reality, but a way of life.

Now, in the rest of the plant, that might be an option. Say you work for a cola company and the leadership goal is to be the "number three cola in the world." Hey, if you can't be Coke or Pepsi, at least compete, right? I mean, it's better than being the number four cola or number fourteen. So in many ways not being number one is still a success because the goal of the number one cola company in this country is so unrealistic for so many. (I mean, look how long it took Coca-Cola to get there.)

But when it comes to safety, number three isn't good enough; it has to be number one, if not company-wide than for each and every individual handling industrial machinery, chemicals, tools, weapons, fireworks, whatever.

Are You a "Problem Avoider" or a "Success Seeker"?

There's a sign hanging somewhere in almost every plant I visit that says something along the lines of, 184 Days without an Accident. And as encouraging as those signs are, they speak to our general, industry-wide attitude about safety, that is, "Look how long it's been since we screwed up."

Just once I'd like to walk into a plant and see a sign that says: "You Are Now Entering a 100 Percent Safe Worksite." Or even, "You Are Now at a Plant That Strives to be 100 Percent Safe."

In other words, rather than being content with simply not getting hurt, we should be striving to be safe. The first is avoiding failure; the second is seeking success.

The problem with leadership attitudes, management mandates, and even warning signage is that if we're not careful, the message of failure avoidance creeps into every other nook and cranny of the site. If leadership sends the message that the only important criterion for determining safety is nobody getting hurt, then everyone will go along with that line of thinking and simply seek not to get hurt.

Which is fine, trust me. But...not getting hurt today often leads to getting hurt tomorrow. If everybody's stepping over that chemical spill simply to save his or her own skin and stay off that sign in the front lobby, then nobody's actually proactively doing anything about, you know, cleaning up that spill.

And just because no one reported an accident tonight doesn't mean machines were running smoothly, spills and cracks and hazards weren't evidenced, and mishaps weren't just narrowly avoided.

There is also the issue of reporting versus solving. When "x amount of days without an accident" becomes the prevailing safety message on site, then everyone kind of works to keep that mandate flowing. So things get pretty dicey when it comes to reporting.

What qualifies as an accident, anyway? Is a broken thumb an accident? A stubbed toe? A chemical burn that doesn't require a trip to the ER? Does it only get reported if a doctor or nurse or hospital or ambulance or fire truck gets involved? Does it only qualify as an accident if the local paper finds out about it?

These are all ways in which accident avoidance morphs and becomes disguised as safety. But really, all we're doing is seeking to avoid failure and creating an unsafe working environment for ourselves and everyone else involved.

Send the Proper Cues (Even If They're Completely Inappropriate!)

When I was in the burn unit, my family would come to see me every day. They had to wear protective clothing from head to toe—gowns, masks, even the little booties on their feet and gloves on their hands. All I could really see were the tears in their eyes as they held my hand through those darkest, earliest days.

Every day they were there at my side. One day my mother came in and said, "Charlie, the guys from work have sent you a gift. Would you like to see it?"

At this point I couldn't speak. I was hooked up to every tube, dial, button, and machine in the hospital, it seemed. I was on my back, arms suspended over my head so that they wouldn't fuse to the rest of my body as they healed.

I could only nod and, with open mouth, make guttural noises. Mom took it as a yes and brought in a large box decked out in wrapping paper and bows.

"Should I open it?" she asked, looking nervously at my father.

I nodded and grunted that she should. When she did, I couldn't contain my laughter: it was a toaster oven! My family was highly offended, and why not? It was absolutely inappropriate and absolutely the best gift I could have ever received at just the right time.

If you work on the line, if you're in our business, you know what I'm talking about. That's how the guys at work were. Later, when I could accept nonfamily visitors, the guys from work would come in and kick my bed, call me a loafer, and tell me nothing was wrong with me.

They had special names for me, too, ones that my family naturally didn't take too kindly to. My favorite, believe it or not, was Krispy Kritter! You know, typical gallows humor just like I would have heard on any work night back on the job.

It was just what I needed—some reality, some humor, the realization that life hadn't stopped for these guys, and that more importantly, my life wasn't over. There was still laughter to be had; life was still worth living.

As much as my family was there in my darkest hours, my friends and coworkers provided an equal amount of TLC in their own grossly inappropriate ways. Both were equally necessary to quite literally save my life. I'll never be able to thank them enough.

So how about your site? How do you handle the "after" protocol of a work-related accident, incident, or report? Trust me, it matters more than you think. One of the best indicators of future success is past performance; your people know this. How you treat safety, and even how you treat those who get injured on the job, is a signal as to how you truly, genuinely feel about safety. You can't hide your true attitude because it will always come out.

If punishment is one of your safety strategies, you're sending the clear message that performance is more important than people. Isn't it? Isn't that what you're saying when you give people demerits or a discipline report because of an incident?

Even if that's not the intention, that's the message people get. You might see it as a deterrent, but people still see it as retribution. That simple disciplinary action screams, "We had a good thing going, Tom. Two hundred and sixty-four days without an incident and you just scrubbed the board back to zero. So, yeah, here's your demerit, and we'll see you back here next month. If you're lucky..."

Again, it's the impersonal approach to safety that so rarely works. Instead, we need to send personal cues—through personal support—when accidents do happen.

I'll never forget the outpouring of genuine, concerned, and sincere affection I felt after my accident. People I hadn't talked to in years sent me cards, stopped my wife in the grocery store, and sent her home with good wishes or a fruit basket or something to make her day a bit brighter.

Sure, Exxon corporate did their best to cover my room in flowers and I was appreciative, but it was the individual efforts of upper management and line supervisors that touched me as powerfully, if not more.

It was the people who showed up to my room, or stopped by my house and said "hi" to my kids, or sent a card or a letter offering help or simply condolences that literally helped save my life.

Recovery is not just a physical process, it's an emotional

one. The guilt I felt, the shame and embarrassment and humiliation and self-doubt and self-hatred I felt were just as painful, if not more, as my intensely horrific physical burns and later my scars.

So much is involved in recovery and so many signals are sent by how you—as a company, a supervisor, a manager or leader, or simply a coworker—treat someone who's injured or reported a hazard or even blown a whistle. If we ignore these people, distrust them or back talk them or gossip about them or shame them or, heaven forbid, punish them, we send a very simple message that is loud and clear: "Safety is number two."

Never underestimate the power of the signals you send. What you do after an accident is just as important as the steps you take to prevent them, because how you treat those who've been injured broadcasts loud and clear how you feel about everyone who works at your company.

"I'm Making This Call Now So I Don't Have to Make Another One Later"

I was at a factory years ago in California. They made silicon, I believe, for computer chips. It was very technical work, very hands-on and labor-intensive, very chemically oriented and dangerous with its own set of hazards and risks.

And yet they had an excellent safety record. I'm talking, the kind you brag about to investors, even customers—that kind of safety record. So I'm talking to the plant manager after my presentation, asking him, "How did you get this safety record?"

He grinned and told me a story that will tell you the kind of extreme measures that are sometimes required to take a personal approach to actual safety.

This plant manager had a guy, one of those Cool Charlie types who never wore his safety equipment or, when he did, only wore half or wore it wrong or just to shut the manager up. (Sound familiar yet?) And no matter how this manager rode the guy, he couldn't get him to comply.

And he knew in his gut, the chemicals this guy was working with, the materials, that he was going to get hurt one day, perhaps permanently. Of course, it was the old catch-22. The plant manager could have fired this guy, but he was a really good worker. And he'd spent hundreds of thousands of dollars on the man's training and orientation; he didn't want to turn around, lose a good guy, and have to train a potentially bad one.

So after one more blowout about this guy not wearing his safety equipment, the plant manager took drastic measures into his own hands. Specifically, he called the guy's wife! And this is what he said: "Ma'am, this is your husband's supervisor. Now, now, nothing's wrong—yet. But ma'am, I need your help. You see, no matter how hard I try, I can't get your husband to wear his safety equipment. And I'm asking you, I'm begging you, to have a word with him. Because if he doesn't wear his safety equipment, I'm afraid one day he's not going to come home to you. So ma'am,

I'm making this call now so I don't have to make another one later..."

True story. And it might not surprise you to learn that after that phone call, that worker wore his safety equipment every day on the job. The plant manager never had to say another word. In fact, neither man ever mentioned the phone call, but the message was loud and clear: "We care about your safety, even if we have to get ruthless about communicating that message to you in a way the guidebooks don't cover."

More simply, this plant manager had quite literally made safety real to this employee and his wife. They both understood the true definition of safety—of going home to your family at the end of each shift.

I'm often asked if I think having the threat of job loss or getting fired over workers' heads is enough to ensure safety. My answer is no. In fact, I never fire anybody for that kind of thing.

I've been a safety guy for years now. I can remember being in charge of the ironworkers at one plant. That was my job: safety manager. That meant I was in charge of managing the safety of my men. It was my job the night a twenty-one-year-old ironworker fell off the scaffolding at my plant and died as a result of his injuries.

There's a sight and a sound I will never forget. It's the sight of that young man's face before they carried him away to the morgue; it's the sound of the zipper on the body bag as they zipped it up for the last time. I swore, then and there, that nothing like that would ever happen again. Not to me and not to anyone on one of my jobs. And still I never fired anybody for not wearing their harnesses.

Even after this young man's coworkers still refused to wear their harnesses after his death. Even after I'd gone to the union and said, "Listen, if you guys don't handle this problem, I will." Even after I handed out verbal warnings and written warnings and the guys still wouldn't wear their harnesses.

My rule was sorely tested one night when I showed up to work, looked up at the scaffolding, and saw all my iron-workers climbing the scaffolding, not a safety harness to be seen.

I quickly called them down and told them quite simply, "Listen, guys, I'm done fighting with you. You don't have to wear your safety harnesses. I'm not going to make you. But just so you know, you can't work here anymore if you don't wear them."

It was a simple choice after that, but a choice just the same.

We Are Family

People often ask what might have gotten me to wear my safety goggles the night of the accident. I know what didn't work because guys had been doing it for years: yelling at me to put my safety goggles on. "Charlie, put your goggles on!" "Charlie, put your helmet on!" "Charlie…"

It got so I never heard what came after my name. That's

what yelling does. You hear it so often, so loudly, it stops having an impact. Plus, it immediately puts the receiver of the command on the defensive.

It's simple human nature—you push me, I'm going to push back. But you don't want to know what wouldn't have worked; you want to know what would have worked.

Well, I can tell you, we have to start caring about each other on the line—not just management and supervisors, but peer to peer. We have to care enough about the guy working next to us to get over our insecurities or our anxiety, and when we see him working without his safety gear, lean over and say something, something real.

If someone had said to me, "Charlie, come on, man. You've got a lovely wife at home waiting on you. You've got two beautiful daughters who look up to you, who need their father. Don't you want to see them when you go home tonight? Well, you can't if you're blind. And that's what can happen if you don't wear your goggles…"

We have to start making it real for them, person to person. That's where safety starts. With you, with me, with the next guy on the line, with family and friends and the people who matter most.

It's behavior, folks. How we behave at home affects how we behave at work. I never drank on the job, but I brought my alcoholic tendencies to work with me every single day.

That behavior, I believe, directly contributed to my accident. The recklessness of drinking, the callousness of not caring about my coworkers, the ambivalence of doing a hard job poorly, the selfishness, the delusion to think, *It'll never happen to me*, were all behaviors and habits forged during years and years of drinking.

So I know firsthand that wherever we go, there we are. If you're reckless doing home repairs, you'll be reckless on the job as well. You ever see a guy whose garage looks as neat, organized, spiffy, and squared away as the showroom floor of a Home Depot? You think that guy's going to suddenly be a sloppy, slovenly, careless slob on the job? It's like with like; he'll be as neat and tidy on the job as he is at home.

What's more, when you're doing this type of work, you can't see the guy on the line next to you as a coworker, he's gotta be a brother. Even if he's the kind of loud, gruff, boisterous, smart-ass brother you love to hate, he's got to be family or you simply won't care enough to reach out to him and say, "Hey, Cliff, come on. What are you doing? You left your goggles at home again? Listen, I care about you and your eyes. I want you to go home and see that beautiful wife of yours after work tonight. I want you to see that son of yours graduate next year. Here, take my extra pair..."

In many plants, there is work and there is safety—like two trains traveling on parallel tracks, they can be right next to each other, but never the two shall meet. We've got to make it so the job is safety and safety is the job.

I remember sitting at home on 9/11, watching the footage of those fearless firemen and cops and EMTs running into those burning towers, one after the other, to save the lives of random strangers. I always marveled at their courage, even more so as I realized that was their job, to go where others feared to tread. They'd signed up for that challenge, been trained every day to do the opposite of how most of us would react.

Now, I'm not asking any of you to run into a burning building, but I'm asking you to consider the lives of yourself and your fellow workers as if they were your own family.

When you do, there will be no question that you'll call them out for not wearing what they should, for rushing through a careful job, or for walking past a dangerous environment. It's easy to ignore the sins of coworkers; it's much harder to ignore the errors your family makes.

Caring Isn't Always Sharing: A Word about Caution

When to rush into a burning building and help?

When to put your emotions behind and use logic to address a potential emergency?

When to slow down rather than speed up?

Is it better to risk two lives rather than one?

These are the kinds of tough safety questions I'm asked every day.

In oil refineries, hydrogen sulfide (or H_2S) leaks are all too common. When I first started out at the Bayonne, New Jersey, refinery, I would often smoke with a bunch of old-timers in what was then known as the "smoker's shed."

One day I was looking out from the shed and saw a man go down next to one of the pipes. I immediately rushed over to help, thinking he'd had a heart attack. One of the old-timers grabbed my collar and yanked me back. "Hang on, kid," he advised. "Put on a pack first and then see what's wrong."

I couldn't believe it. Didn't these guys want to help a fellow worker? A fallen comrade? But I did as I was told and suited up, and by the time I got there, several other employees in safety suits were already there. Sure enough, the man had died from an H_2S leak.

If I'd rushed in without protection, without wearing my pack as the old-timer had advised, I'd have been dead right along with him. It reminded me of my days as a volunteer fireman. Invariably we'd race to a burning building, and all of us youngbloods would leap off the truck and race straight toward the flames.

And yet again, another old-timer would grab us by the collar and remind us, "Get your gear on first; then rush into the burning building. Otherwise one of us is going to have to risk our butts to come in and save you as well."

So there is a real need for logic as well as emotion. We need to feel for our fellow workers as if they are family, but care for ourselves enough to protect ourselves. No one's telling you not to help your fellow man, but don't risk your own life to do it. Follow procedure, wear your gear, wait for help, or be in a position to give real help, not just emotional help.

If you run into a burning building knowing nothing more than the guy you're trying to rescue, what good are you to him? What good are you to yourself? He might be even more experienced than you, about to escape, and here you are, putting your own self at risk, and he'll die trying to save you?

Help as much as you can when you can, but never sacrifice safety for heroism. Sometimes emotion needs to take a backseat to reason, to rationale, and to process.

Making Safety a Personal Priority

It's time to put the personal back into personal priority when it comes to safety. It can't just be numbers and facts, buzzwords and figures, charts and graphs.

There were 1,200 employees at my Exxon plant when we got a new plant manager, John Race, many years ago. Morale at Exxon was low at the time, and John had just been reassigned to our refinery as a result of some personnel shuffling in the wake of the *Exxon Valdez* tanker spill.

Not long after he arrived John asked me into his office. I was the union safety rep at the time, so part of my job was walking the thin line between making management happy and caring for the front line, hard-core union shop guys.

John knew I spoke for the plant's rank and file when he asked me, "Charlie, is there anything I can do to increase morale around the plant? I mean, I'm new here, our numbers are down, confidence is low, I need to send a clear and strong message that I'm here to make some changes in a nonthreatening way."

Now, it was getting close to the holidays around that

time. I gave John two pieces of advice that day. "Years ago," I told him, "we used to hang Christmas lights from the tanks. We had five tanks, and they'd hang the lights so they looked like five giant Christmas trees as you entered and left the plant. Folks could see them from the road. They discontinued the practice during the energy crisis, but if I were you, I'd bring them back."

John gave me a kind of puzzled look. I think he was expecting something a little more effective than Christmas lights. He said, "I can do that, Charlie. What else?"

"Also," I told him, "you've got to can that xeroxed Christmas letter you send out every year. 'Dear Employee, Merry Christmas.' Send folks an actual card addressed to them."

Finally John smiled. "Charlie, I'll go you one better. My wife Betty and I will personally sign every Christmas card."

We left on good terms, and what's more, John was as good as his word. The lights went up, and it was a really big deal. Then the Christmas cards started arriving, and sure enough, John and his wife Betty signed each and every one—all 1,200 of them!

Shortly after the New Year, John called me back into his office to thank me for my advice. He said, "Charlie, I can't believe it. I've never gotten as big a response from such simple steps in my life. I could have given the entire plant a raise and not achieved the same results. I got more thank-you letters, more phone calls at home and here in the office, than I could have ever imagined…"

John Race was surprised that such simple results could mean so much to so many. I wasn't. I'd already seen first-hand the personal way so many of the plant's employees had responded with kindness, with flowers, with cards, with letters and phone calls after my accident.

I already knew that if you make safety personal, they will come…

Office Safety: It's Not Just about You

Now, I know what you're thinking: what could possibly go wrong in an office setting, right? I mean, what can I tell you from my experience in an oil refinery that could possibly apply to office safety?

What can happen, am I right? Are you going to stab yourself with a pencil? Get third-degree rug burns? A three-alarm trash can fire? A life-threatening paper cut?

Let's face it, you and I both know there aren't a lot of big-time safety hazards lurking around the typical office. There are no incendiary desks, no radioactive file cabinets, no poisoned pens, so what could possibly go wrong?

And I'll admit, on the surface of it, office safety is not a major issue. I can tell you, not a lot of insurance agencies or editorial departments are clamoring for my services as a safety consultant, if you get my drift.

What's more, you're probably thinking that the few things you can do to stay safe in your office you can do blindfolded, backward and forward, up and down in your sleep. I get it, I really do. Because that's exactly what I was thinking the night I nearly blew myself to kingdom come.

Are You an Accident Waiting to Happen?

Being an operator at an oil refinery, I had to work in a lot of dangerous situations, but the night of my accident wasn't one of them. In fact, the job I was doing that night was as routine as you could get, something I'd done a thousand times before.

The only difference was, that night I was taking shortcuts and plenty of them. I was so on autopilot that I barely knew what I was doing other than hurrying up to finish my shift and get to my family in our little rented cottage on the beach so I could start my vacation.

You could say I was already on vacation. It wasn't the hazardousness of the job that night that got me; it was the arrogance and the apathy of my attitude that got me.

I was quite literally an accident waiting to happen. But this chapter isn't about me, it's about you. So let me ask you a few questions to get started:

- Have you ever rushed a job so you could get off work early?
- Have you ever skipped a few steps in any procedure to just get it over with?
- Have you ever left something unfinished, figuring someone else will take care of that?

- Do you consider safety management's job?
- Or the safety department's job?
- Have you ever taken your job for granted?
- Have you ever taken safety for granted?
- Have you ever taken life for granted?

Look, this is an open-book test, *your* open-book test, so don't lie to me and certainly don't lie to yourself. If you're anything like 99 percent of the thousands of people I talk to every year, if you're brutally honest with yourself, I know you answered "yes" to at least two or three of the above questions.

And that's two or three too many.

Idiot Proofing Your World

People often ask me, "Charlie, between you and me, don't you secretly blame Exxon for what happened to you? I mean, if they'd changed the valves out, the accident wouldn't have happened, right?"

Do I wish the valves had been changed out earlier? That they weren't so hard to open or close? That the procedure would have taken ten minutes rather than forty minutes? Sure, of course I do.

But the valves were old, they were hard to open and close, and the procedures worked, even if they did take forty minutes to perform properly. Those are the facts.

Here's another fact: there isn't a single facility on the

planet, bar none, that is 100 percent safe 100 percent of the time. Every work site, every home, has some safety issue just waiting to change your life.

Just living in this world is unsafe. There are broken white lines on every highway. They're supposed to prevent cars from changing lanes without the driver looking first. They're supposed to protect us, but people disobey the rule anyway; they're in a hurry, they're busy, they're distracted on the phone or yelling at the kids or changing the radio dial, and they change lanes without looking. And there we are, right next to them, minding our own business.

It's not our fault, but there we are just the same, in an accident. We have two choices in that scenario:

1. We can blame the world for our problems and drive just as recklessly, as carelessly, as everybody else.

2. Or…we can know the world is a dangerous, imperfect, unsafe place and simply wear our seat belts.

There's a term out there that I don't particularly care for, though I recognize its accuracy. When we say a procedure is "idiotproof," we mean that anyone can do it. We imply that it's so simple, it's practically error-free.

It's a way to make the world safe for everyone all the time. But really? There's no such thing as idiot proofing the world. If you don't believe me, just look at your next cup of drive-through coffee. There are more warning labels on the cup than the fast-food restaurant's logo: "CAUTION: Contents may be hot." Really? Thanks for that completely unnecessary warning label.

But the fact is, someone, somewhere got hurt by drinking their hot coffee too soon or dropping it in their lap or spilling it on their hands, and so in an effort to idiot proof their cups, the restaurant added a warning label or two or three or four.

Along those same lines, I think the best sign we're trying maybe a little too hard to create an idiotproof world is the warning I saw on the outside of a pizza box recently: "Open box before eating pizza." Seriously, this warning exists.

I guess the point I'm trying to make is that at some point we have to stop waiting for the world to protect us and get up off our butts and protect ourselves. So what if the valves were old, if they were hard to open and the procedure took awhile? It was what it was, and that was the job I was paid to do. I should have done it right the first time.

Every job site, every home, will have risk involved. Our job is to avoid the risk by following procedures simply and safely. If you want to idiot proof safety, then simple do the right job at the right time the right way. See how simple that was?

But simple isn't enough; responsibility is. I do a lot of work speaking to railroad companies, talking to their employees about safety. And I learned recently that the railroads are considering putting up giant nets at the railroad crossings. "Why?" you might ask. The reason is simple: people keep driving around the gates.

Forget they're blocking the road, forget they're blinking red and green, forget there's a giant, speeding train blowing its horn bearing right down on them; people keep driving around the gates and getting hit by trains.

And so...what? Nets are going to stop them? That's the problem with safety: when we take personal responsibility out of the equation, what we put in its place are practices and procedures and solutions that are often bizarre in the lengths they go to apologize for basic human stupidity.

We don't need nets at railroad crossings; we need people to stop driving around the gates we have now. It's very simple—first and foremost, time and time again, safety is about personal responsibility.

It's not easy because human nature is to make things as difficult as possible. But safety is simple; we just have to take responsibility for our own actions.

Playing the Odds

I know what you're thinking right now: *I work in an office, Charlie. What's the worst that can happen to me if I don't follow safety procedures?*

It's a good question, and you'll be happy to know that the answer is, quite frankly, "Nine out of ten times, nothing will happen to you." Let's face it, it's probably more like ninety-nine times out of one hundred nothing will happen.

But can you afford to take the risk? Can you afford to play those odds? Let me put it another way: Can your family, your spouse, your kids, your loved ones? Can the people who care about you most afford to go on without you?

You know what the most dangerous jobs on the planet are? The ones you've rushed through and skimped on a thousand times before and gotten away with. If you're nervous about skipping steps on the job or ignoring protocol or procedure, and somebody says to you, "Don't worry. We've skipped this step a thousand times before, and nobody's gotten hurt yet...," look out; those are the real dangerous jobs.

Like mine. I'd always, always gotten away with closing one valve instead of two when switching out blanks at the refinery—until the night I didn't get away with it. And trust me, it only takes that once. It only takes one skipped step, one rushed procedure, one look away or bit of multitasking when you should be focusing to change your life forever.

People often ask me what the worst part of my accident was. Was it the scars, the pain, the hearing loss, or clouded vision? Was it the hit my reputation took, or even my income?

It was none of those things. I was thirty-three at the time of my accident. I had a wife and two daughters; they were ten and fifteen at the time. And for the next five years, I was in the hospital. First it was the burn unit, then it was inpatient rehab, then it was outpatient, and then it was for this corrective surgery or that nip or that tuck.

And so for five years, I wasn't there for my daughters. I missed their games, their awards, their concerts, and their lives. To you and me, as grown adults, five years doesn't mean all that much. A few more gray hairs, a few more pounds around the middle, a laugh line here or there—that's about it.

To a kid growing up, five years is everything. Every friend is your best friend. Every song is your new anthem. Every heartbreak is the end all and be all of your existence. Every pimple is a tragedy; every A plus is a triumph.

And I missed it all. My daughters went from being young girls to young adults while I was on operating table after operating table undoing the damage I myself had caused through my own carelessness, arrogance, and false pride.

You know, it wasn't even that. What it boils down to, the fight between me and my safety equipment, was a lot less complicated: I wanted to be comfortable, period.

My safety goggles were big and bulky and didn't look very macho. The sleeves of my flame-retardant shirt were bulky and hot, and it was summer so I had them rolled up to my shoulders.

My gloves were hot and heavy and would only get in the way. And my hard hat? Please! This wasn't a construction site, and besides, I was very particular about my hair.

So that's the gamble I took that night, comfort over safety. And it was my girls who really lost in the end. All the pain and tragedy and agony and heartache I experienced, I'd go through it all over again—a million times over, and I mean that—if I could just get those five years with my daughters back.

If I could just sit there in my favorite chair and smile

obligingly as they gushed about this new boyfriend or that new pair of jeans or this new album or that new movie I just had to take them to. If I could watch them grow up, year after year, rather than look up one day to find that my girls had grown up without me even being around.

Do you know what it's like to say good-bye to your two young daughters one warm August night only to walk back through the door five years later and find they've grown up, and moved on, without you?

New hairstyles, new cheekbones, each a foot taller and with new friends, new clothes, new styles, and new personalities? It was like being frozen in ice while the rest of the world moved on without me.

So let me ask you one more question: are you willing to take that risk?

Always Simple, but Never Easy

The tragedy of workplace accidents is how simple they are to avoid and yet how frequently they occur. I think that's because we often equate simplicity with ease.

It's very simple to turn off the office coffeepot every night, and it's real easy to forget when you're rushing out the door at a quarter to five, eager to beat the traffic so you can get home and defrost the ground chuck before the rest of the family gets home.

And so what happens when that coffeepot has sat on that hot burner all night, one night too many? So you brew a fresh pot the next morning, smiling at your mistake, and when you go to pour your first cup of the day, just as you have a million and one times before, crack goes the bottom of that compromised pot and scalding hot coffee burns your arms, your legs, your midsection, wherever it hits. And because of a simple error in judgment, a simple gambling of the odds—oh, this old coffeepot is indestructible, it'll last forever—there you are, scarred for life.

And maybe you don't need to miss five years of your child's life; maybe you only need to miss one or two for all those skin grafts, the rehab, and the corrective plastic surgeries.

Really? Is there a parent on this planet who would willingly give up one or two years of their children's lives for mere convenience? Not the parents I know.

And it can happen just like that. If you don't believe me, just look at your office with an objective eye. Take that filing cabinet over there, for instance.

The edges don't look that sharp, do they? But now imagine rushing in from the other room, vision obscured by a stack of file folders as you trip on the seam in the carpet and go slamming into that cabinet corner face-first.

Do you lose an eye? Or just have an unsightly scar on your forehead for the rest of your life? Is either worth the extra time it would have taken you to make two trips to retrieve those folders, if only so you could see where you were going and not trip over the carpet seam?

Hiding in Plain Sight

If anything, office safety is vitally important simply because we think it's such a joke. You walk onto the floor of a chemical plant, and let me tell you, it's intimidating. You want to wear your safety equipment once you see all that heavy machinery, all those gurgling pots of chemical goo, and get one whiff of all those nasty toxins.

You work in an oil refinery, and it's not hard to see the dangers lurking around every corner. Same with a warehouse full of big machinery or a plant loaded with hissing engines and grinding gears and fiery furnaces and molten metal. The more dangerous a place looks, the easier it is to motivate folks to follow safety procedures.

But the dangers in your typical office? I like to say they're hiding in plain sight. That's because, as I also like to say, stuff happens even in safe places.

Case in point: I recently read the tragic story of a young woman who took a shortcut around the office with dire consequences. It was something she'd done a million times before, something you've probably done a million times before as well.

The young woman in question was an administrative assistant. She had only one thing left on her to-do list before she could head home and that was merely to transfer some files from her office to the storage center downstairs.

It was late, close to quitting time, and she wanted to save herself an extra trip so she overstuffed the box with one too many files and headed for the elevator. Well, of course it was running slow that day, with everyone in the office trying to get home early and beat the traffic.

So this young woman decided to use the stairs. She got about halfway down when her heel got caught in the hem of her dress. The weight from the box of files gave her momentum, and without any way to balance herself, she went smashing face-first into the concrete wall.

She destroyed half her face that day, and all she was carrying was paper. All she wanted to do was save herself a few minutes by carrying twice as many files.

But instead of saving herself a few minutes, she spent the next few months in the hospital as doctors tried to reconstruct her face. She put herself and her family through hell, and I can tell you from experience, it's still not over.

Freak accident, right? Could never happen to you. Let me tell you about a sales rep for a packaging company. For years she worked in the safe, comfortable confines of the main office just on the other side of the factory.

That didn't exactly mean she was a stranger to the factory floor. Several times a day she had to cross the factory to get coffee and meet with people from various departments. Occasionally she'd stop to watch the workers on the production line.

She liked the way they all pulled together, keeping an eye out for a steady work flow. Occasionally she'd seen the boxes on the line jam up against one another, clogging production. With a quick jiggle or stab, one of the workers would get the boxes aligned again and the line would start running smoothly.

One day as she crossed the factory floor, she noticed the boxes had jammed up on the line again. She kind of peered around to spot a worker, but no one was around. He must have gone on break.

She got a little nervous. I mean, the line was waiting for the boxes to flow, and there they were, a logjam in process and it would only get worse. Where could that line worker be?

She faced a dilemma. It wasn't her job and it was far out of her skill set, but should she lean over and poke the boxes as she'd seen the workers do a thousand times before to get the line going? Or should she ignore the problem and keep going? After all, it wasn't her department. Technically, she probably shouldn't do anything about it. What if she screwed things up?

She shrugged and decided to give the boxes a push. *How hard could it be?* she thought to herself, approaching the line cautiously. You give the boxes a push, and they go down the line. Simple as can be.

But she never made it that far. The minute she reached out to touch the boxes, she triggered a sensor that alerted a metal cutting arm to engage; it did so immediately, cutting her arm right off.

What had looked so simple to the untrained eye was actually a maneuver fraught with danger, one the men who so dutifully worked the line had been trained in and drilled over countless times before.

She hadn't stepped in to adjust the boxes at the point the trained workers normally did, a sensor-free area they knew was perfectly safe. Nor did she read the warning signs posted along the conveyor belt, clearly stating where to stand and where not to stand—ever. She didn't know about the emergency off button right below the conveyor belt.

God bless her, she had no idea—could never imagine in a million years—that an electric eye would mistake her arm for a box and signal the metal wrap function to begin. Despite having worked at the factory for years, she was totally unaware of the particular dangers of this one very specific job.

She was an office worker, and office workers usually don't think of the dangers inherent in factory work. Office workers don't normally do dangerous jobs and are unprepared for the specific dangers of each one.

Factory workers often do dangerous jobs but amazingly are rarely hurt by those dangerous jobs. Any idea why? That's right, because their awareness of the danger they face is already heightened. They train for those dangerous jobs, know the dangers, and follow procedures and/or rules to avoid them.

It's the low-risk, low-impact, day in, day out jobs that will kill you!

Accidents Are "Collar Blind"

One of the hardest parts of my recovery was not the physical pain I endured, the shame of what I'd done to my family, or the years I lost while my daughters grew up without me.

As painful and tragic as those aspects of my recuperation were, I think one of the toughest things I had to go through was the realization of how many people just like you and me get hurt in this country every day.

It's kind of like a veil was lifted for me, a hazy veil of false security that said, "It will never happen to me." I think that veil exists for so many of us simply because we've never experienced danger firsthand.

Or we've experienced it but always pulled through without a scratch. What you learn in recovery from an industrial accident, however, is that people hurt themselves every day. And I say "hurt themselves" because, like Princess Diana's senseless death, so many of our own accidents are easily avoidable.

None of the people I was in recovery with were the victims of an industrial accident. No one else came in with chemical burns or missing limbs from heavy machinery on a factory floor. Instead, all were regular workaday people who got hurt doing the most mundane things imaginable.

How many rooms did I share with weekend warriors who had blinded themselves while mowing their own lawns without safety goggles? How many people did I see with arms and legs amputated while doing routine household chores that simply went wrong?

Of all the people I saw during my five years of recovery from my own accident, most of them—*most of them*—were office workers. Most of them had white-collar jobs. The assumption is that the most dangerous jobs result in the most common accidents, but this simply isn't the case. In fact, when it comes to workplace safety, accidents are "collar blind."

In other words, a person with a white collar can get just as seriously injured as a person with a blue collar. The harsh truth is, office workers can be more susceptible to accidents simply because safety isn't drilled into them day in and day out.

Parting Words about Safety on the Job: Carol's Story

I met Carol a few years ago, and I'm proud and honored to call her my friend. Carol's husband Joe died in an industrial accident. And he wasn't doing one of the more typically dangerous jobs at the plant. Joe was an engineer who fell twenty feet to his death through some ductwork he was inspecting.

Carol returned to Joe's facility with her sons to share with Joe's coworkers the impact of that accident—on herself, on her boys, on her family, and the shattered lives Joe left behind.

Like me, Carol has chosen to channel her grief for something positive to come out of her husband's death. She can't bring him back, but she can honor his legacy by speaking about industrial accidents and the loved ones that injured or deceased workers leave behind.

I appreciate Carol's perspective because she speaks from the other side of the coin that I do. I can only speak of my loss, of the pain I imagine my family to have felt while I was in recovery and emotionally and physically abandoned them.

When I hear Carol speak, I imagine what my ex-wife might say if she could talk to me about those lost and painful years. In Carol's words I hear the unspoken truths my daughters are perhaps too anxious, too nervous, too polite to say to me.

And when I see the pain etched in Carol's face or on the faces of her four sons, I often picture Joe heading off to work that fateful day of his accident. He probably never thought twice about where he was going that day or what he'd be doing.

He was an engineer, the office job of all office jobs. Logic, reason, numbers, facts, angles, physics—these are the tools an engineer uses. He was well versed in all of those, just not in safety. And he paid the ultimate price.

Don't let the presumed safety of your job make you blind to the risks of any job. There is danger all around you, if only you'll open your eyes and take the time to see the risk.

If not for yourself, then do it for your family.

CHAPTER 11

The Nine Rules of Safety

I watch TV differently now. I read the news and listen to the radio and sit in movie theaters differently now, too. I can't help it. It's hard to watch a movie where there are explosions and fire and not think about the victims left behind in the rubble as the hero or heroine races ahead to save the day.

I get preoccupied with what's going to happen to them or would if this was real life. With the burns and the scars and the painful surgeries and years of intense physical therapy and restriction of movement, I can't help it.

It happens every year: the holidays roll around and every news channel, it seems, features the same stories about folks trying to fry turkeys in their homes. Yes, you heard right: inside their homes. Or their garages or under an awning or in a work shed.

And I watch the news footage of the smoldering house after the fire department has left and the family has moved into a hotel room with what's left of their belongings, and I think of who might have gotten hurt and how badly and what's in store for them.

And then I get a little mad because...seriously? There are accidents, and then there are invitations. You fry a turkey in an industrial kitchen with a fire extinguisher every two inches and a wire shorts and ignites the oil, that's an accident. You fry a turkey in a vat of oil inside your own home, and that's an invitation.

Safety isn't hard, but it's real easy to forget. Accidents happen, and they happen in an instant. I think of my friend Courtney from rehab—the one who dressed up as a mummy for her sorority party and backed into a lit cigarette, and instantly, her entire life changed. One second she has her whole future ahead of her; the next she is burned over 90 percent of her body.

In rehab, the rooms are very spartan: bed, nightstand, lamp, water bottle—period. There wasn't a lot of room for family pictures or mementos on the bedside table, and I was always kind of happy about that. Not for myself so much—I loved looking at pictures of my daughters and gaining inspiration from their happier, earlier smiling faces.

But I worried that in trying to comfort her with the old and familiar, Courtney's parents might put old family photos by the bed, pictures of a younger Courtney before the fire.

Her graduation picture, perhaps, all that unblemished skin and a smile that didn't know pain and eyes that didn't know the hopeless depths of all the long, endless nights to come.

Back in rehab, I felt more guilty about my accident than

sorry for it. Unlike Courtney, I knew it was my fault. I knew that pissed as I was about the situation, I only had myself to blame. I had invited my accident, plain and simple.

Sometimes, through sloppiness, arrogance and thoughtlessness, we cause our own accidents. An obvious example is not asking someone to hold the ladder steady while you hang the Christmas lights because you're too tough or macho or just want to get it done. The consequences could be disastrous.

A much worse example is driving through a red light because you're texting someone about something that will never be as important as the horror you can bring upon yourself and someone else by this inexcusable behavior.

Wrapping yourself in toilet paper on Halloween night and thinking you'll laugh over all your goofy pictures the next morning, not wind up in a burn unit, is an example of a truly tragic accident where the victim did not act irresponsibly. She just made a poor choice that nearly killed her.

I guess my point is, life is too precious to ignore safety, even in the "safe" moments when you think nothing bad can ever, or will ever, happen to you or your loved ones.

What's Your Culture Like?

I talk a lot about culture when I speak at companies all over the world. That's because every company has a culture; so does every home. It's that attitude, that general tone, that reveals what's really important to a person, a boss, an employee, or a plant.

At Exxon, there was a prevalent culture of safety. I just didn't respect and/or appreciate it. I was like the kid with two left feet lurking in the shadows at the high school dance. Everyone else got it but me.

What does your workplace culture say about your company's attitude toward safety? Oftentimes, the actual culture of a site is at odds with what the company says its culture is.

In other words, you can have safety signs and equipment and warnings up the wazoo, but if you're careless or lax about safety, then on the line, in the actual workplace, from the leadership to management to your supervisor to your coworkers on down, the message is clear: "Safety is number two."

It happens a lot. I see it in a lot of the organizations that invite me to speak to them. I'm never sure if they're inviting me to speak to satisfy some workplace quota of safety initiatives, because they know they have a problem and want to fix it or want to check off another box on their safety to-do list.

Regardless of the reason, I don't change my message when I'm in front of an audience, any audience. And I can often sense the culture even as I'm led around the plant before or after my presentation. It's in the quality, or even the condition, of the equipment in the plant, the attitudes of the workers, the cleanliness of the site.

I can even tell when a supervisor or management is uneasy or unfamiliar on the plant floor, as if it's the first time they've walked around the production or line for quite some time. It's hard to be concerned about on-the-line safety when you're rarely on the line.

At home, culture comes from the top down. How do the parents feel about safety? That's how the kids will feel about safety. Are there pesticides and household cleaners on the bottom shelf, where any old kid with a curious imagination can get into them, expecting to taste blue raspberry when he takes a swallow of window cleaner? Are there guards on the outlets, a gate around the pool, a lock on the gun cabinet? These daily habits, these small but significant safety measures tell me—tell your kids—a lot about the culture of safety in your home.

Again, it comes down to a question of culture, which comes from the top down. If safety isn't important to the big boss, it's not going to be important to the VP, management, or your supervisor. That's why any safety initiative has to be fully endorsed company-wide and not in just one isolated department or as the sole cause of a single supervisor.

Safety happens when it's a habit, not a holiday or onetime occurrence. One of the reasons I'm so passionate when I speak is because I'm afraid that it could be that plant's one and only shot at taking safety seriously, and I don't want to blow it.

Like the supervisors at Exxon who were forever nagging me to wear my hard hat, gloves, or safety goggles, I know I may be the only voice in the room making safety count, so I try to make an impact in the little time I have.

The Nine Rules of Safety

Safety doesn't have to be so complicated. In fact, it's very simple. It starts today and continues tomorrow, and the safer you are, the safer you'll always be. But you have to start somewhere.

This chapter is a good start. That's because the nine rules of safety that follow are designed to help make safety a part of every day, at every company, in every home.

THE FIRST RULE OF SAFETY: BE AWARE

Safety starts with awareness, period. If you're not aware of your surroundings, you're simply not being safe. That's why culture is such a big part of it. The more a company's culture revolves around safety, the more aware everyone is, all the time.

Management shares the culture with HR, and HR shares it with new hires, but that's the formal culture. The real test is on the line, where the culture lives or dies. Good or bad, the old guys share that culture with the new guys, who in turn pass it on when they have the chance.

If it's a culture of safety, that message permeates from day one of a new hire's time punch. Same with a reckless culture; new hires pick up on it right away and it's hard to unring that bell.

And here's where awareness comes in. In a culture of safety, awareness is like elevator music—you may not hear it or pay attention to every song as you ride up or down, but it's there in the background just the same.

You may not clock in consciously thinking, *I'm at work; I need to start being aware now*. It's just there, like the low hum of machinery in the background or the way your eyes kind of look around every few minutes to take in your surroundings.

If I'd been more aware on the night of my accident, I would have avoided years of pain and heartache for me and my family. More specifically, I would have followed procedures. Not because it was a particularly risky job, but because I'd have been aware that every job was risky and that's why there were procedures in the first place.

Awareness seeps into every area of your life on and off the job. You're more aware of dangerous drivers on the way to and from work, of the need for your entire family to wear their seat belts, of the warning labels on your Christmas lights and new chainsaw.

THE SECOND RULE OF SAFETY: BE PREPARED

With awareness comes preparation, both on the part of each company and its employees. New equipment requires new procedures. Older equipment requires even more procedures!

One of the reasons I cut corners on the night of my accident was specifically because the old blanks I was supposed to be switching out required lots more TLC than newer ones. I simply couldn't be bothered to be aware, prepared, *or* careful.

But Exxon was prepared; they had specific procedures in place because those blanks were old. And once they got replaced, Exxon would have specific procedures to be prepared for those.

What's more, preparation is a before, during, and after event. Procedures prepare you before a job, habits and skill and awareness and dozens of other factors help you be prepared during, and after an event there should be protocols in place that let everyone know what to do in case of an emergency.

THE THIRD RULE OF SAFETY: BE VIGILANT

Vigilance is everyone's job, on site or off. My buddy's wife tells him every time he leaves the house, "Drive defensively." What she means, of course, is that you can't trust anybody to look out for you out there, so you have to look out for yourself.

She means stay away from that potential drunk driver who keeps inching over into your lane and the teen texting while driving and the blue hair you can't see over the steering wheel.

It may not be fair to have to watch out for your driving *and* everyone else's on the road, but there it is. Fair or not, to not be vigilant would be to invite an accident through no fault of your own.

The same is even more true on the job. How many guys had to be extra vigilant when old macho Charlie was on shift, with his flame-retardant sleeves rolled up and safety goggles hanging from the rearview mirror in his truck? How many times did an unknown and unseen coworker save my butt, and his own, by being vigilant when I was being reckless?

Just like on the road, you can't just look out for yourself when you're at work or on the line. You've got to be vigilant about not just your own safety, but the next guy's and the next guy's.

Likewise, a supervisor needs to be vigilant about the safety of his team, and management needs to be vigilant about the safety of their supervisors, and leaders need to be vigilant about their managers, and so on. It only works if everybody is on board, so the more people who can be vigilant, the safer any environment is going to be.

THE FOURTH RULE OF SAFETY: BE PROACTIVE

Don't just think about safety; **do safety.** It's too easy to post a poster, a sign, a warning, or a list of procedures and then forget about it until the next safety incident. Being proactive means getting involved, getting interested, and participating in not just your own safety but the safety of others.

If you see a hazard, report it. If you don't think current procedures are adequate enough for your own protection, speak up. If you think you can do it, say it, or post it better, say so.

I don't believe that any workplace sets out to be unsafe purposefully. Why would you? So how does it happen? How does a brand-new site, line, piece of equipment, or entire crew become unsafe? One word: **indifference.**

Day by day, little by little, be it from on high or just one pay grade up, safety just kind of gets frittered away. Productivity gets behind, profits sag, things get kicked up a notch, and safety is usually one of the first things to get left behind.

If nobody says anything the first time it happens, it'll just happen sooner the next time and faster the time after that. After a while, safety is so far back in the rearview mirror, you can hardly see it anymore. And by then, it's too late.

Don't let it happen like that. Don't let safety erode into negligence, and whatever you do, don't be actively responsible for letting it reach that point. Instead, be proactive about safety from the beginning.

THE FIFTH RULE OF SAFETY: BE PRESENT

One of the biggest enemies of safety, in addition to indifference, is distraction. We've all been there—not enough sleep the night before, too many shifts in a row, radio on too loud, Excedrin hasn't kicked in yet, horsing around with the guys, and . . . accident in three, two, one.

It's nobody's fault; it's everybody's fault. Trouble is,

none of us can afford to be distracted for too long, too often—if at all. When you're on the job, be on the job. Breakroom, office birthday party, Fourth of July picnic, whatever, be distracted.

On the line, on site, on the job, be present. Like I said, it's not always easy, but it's very simple.

THE SIXTH RULE OF SAFETY: BE REASONABLE

Let's face it, some jobs are just more dangerous than others. If you don't believe me, just ask an ice road trucker or a crab fisherman or a cop or a fireman or a trapeze artist.

Some jobs require more training than others, and yes, a lot of that training will be in the form of safety classes. It only stands to reason that the more hazardous the job, the more rigorous the training should be.

One problem I see in some organizations is the battle over extremes. You've got guys like I used to be, pooh-poohing safety and creating risk, and guys on the completely opposite end of the spectrum who can barely move because they're so extra-cautious about making one wrong move.

The goal should be a balance somewhere between being so hypervigilant you can't perform the job and so careless that, frankly, you shouldn't be on the job.

As I'll mention in a moment, the role of the workplace isn't to be a padded warehouse where no one can get hurt. It's to do good work safely so that nobody should get hurt.

If everyone on the job has reasonable expectations of safety and acts reasonably to ensure that safety, everybody wins.

THE SEVENTH RULE OF SAFETY: BE REALISTIC

Look, work has to be done; I get that. Your company's not in the safety professor business of teaching you how to put on your hard hat or safety goggles every hour on the hour. But...every work site has the responsibility of providing a safe environment for its employees, 24/7/365.

When done right, safety should be background music, not front and center. It should be built in to the culture of the company, the workplace, or even the home, and it should be a constant flow running through the site. That's how it should work.

And that's how it did work at Exxon. Safety was cultivated, the steps were in place, the posters and placards and warnings were everywhere. This was a chemical plant; we had to be safe to do our jobs properly. But I'm living proof that it only takes being careless one time to nearly destroy a life—and an entire plant.

The fact is, we all have to be realistic about safety. It's very simple to do things right; it's even simpler to do them wrong. But either way, we can only hold the company responsible for so much. When given the tools, we must create the safety habit for ourselves.

When the tools aren't there, let's fight for a safe workplace until they are. As much as it's the company's responsibility to provide you with a safe site, it's also your responsibility to ensure that the site is safe.

THE EIGHTH RULE OF SAFETY: BE VOCAL

Speak up; be vocal. If you see someone being a clown on site, call them on it. Let them know you're watching. Let others know you're watching as well.

Don't be the Cool Charlie of your plant, or even your home, sunglasses on so no one knows you're asleep, arms crossed, shaking your head or grunting at every new idea, procedure, or guideline. Be the Careful Charlie who knows it's more macho to save a friend's life, even your own life or the lives of your family, by telling him to knock it off than it is to just go with the flow.

Nearly every day at the plant, some manager or buddy was riding me: "Charlie, pull down your sleeves," "Charlie, put on your safety goggles," "Charlie, where's your hat?," "Where are your gloves?"

After a while, it was almost like a game. They said it with a frown, and I ignored it with a smile. Have you ever seen those Charlie Brown TV specials, where the adult voices are kind of just like a blur and you can't tell what they're saying? That's what I heard when anyone tried to talk to me about safety—an annoying blur.

I never put it together that those guys were actually trying to save my life. At least, not until it was too late.

THE NINTH RULE OF SAFETY: BE VISIBLE

If you're serious about safety, you need to make it clear that safety really *is* number one. Part of being vigilant is also being visible. That means stating, publishing, and posting all procedures and guidelines throughout the plant in real time, in realistic places where workers can see them and understand them.

For instance, here are a few ideas:

1. **Publish the safety procedures far and wide.** If they're different for every department—office, reception, warehouse, production, line—post the appropriate procedures for each department. Line guys don't care about coffeepot safety, and office staff don't need hard hats! Most sites have a wall or a space, where every procedure known to man, from how to file a workman's comp claim to how to drive a forklift, is all posted willy-nilly in the same spot. That's fine if it meets the bare minimum for OSHA, but don't stop there. Post the coffeepot safety guidelines...behind, above, or at least near the coffeepot, and not just for one coffeepot, but all of them. Post the forklift procedures where you keep the forklifts, where the forklift drivers change, and so on. Make them clear, plentiful, and above all visible.

2. **Make sure they're visible and easy to see/read.** Do they have pictures? Are the pictures easy to un-

derstand? Big enough? Accurate enough? This also includes having signs that speak the language. If you have other nationalities working for you, relying on pictures isn't enough. Print the steps of each procedure in as many languages as are spoken at the plant.

3. **Include a safety tip or reminder in every employee newsletter.** What kind of safety tips am I talking about? This can include things like one-line reminders of actual site procedures, such as "Hard hats must be worn at all times." Or it can be a paragraph or two about why safety is important. It can be quotes from actual employees on safety or excerpts from a magazine, book, or newspaper having to do with safety. The contents are just as important as the regularity; if you put out a newsletter weekly, have a "safety section" specifically for these tips. Put it in the same spot each week so folks know to look for it. If you don't have an employee newsletter, start one. If you don't start one, post the tip on the employee's pay envelope! Don't just post some signs and let them gather dust. Make safety a daily responsibility of everyone on site with diligent and brief reminders.

The Best Kind of Hero (Is Not What You Think)

People often come up to me after a speaking engagement and, inspired by my life after my accident, call me a hero. Wow. I couldn't disagree more. I'm not a hero; I've never been a hero. At best, at the time of the accident, I was **stupid**, **careless**, and **selfish**. That's the truth, no smoke and mirrors.

You know what a hero is? I mean, a real hero? A *real* hero is someone who approaches risk with forethought, logic, training, and preparation. That's a hero. Those guys who ran into the burning buildings on 9/11? They were trained to do that; that was their job. They became heroes the day they signed up to run toward danger while everyone was running away, and 9/11 just put them in the spotlight for it. But to them, it was just another day.

What's heroic is that they came prepared with backup, with equipment, with training, with a plan. A hero? I'm no hero. I'd have considered myself a hero if instead of rushing out to that pipeline joint half-cocked and in a hurry, I'd been boring, safe, and predictable by, you know, actually following procedures. That would have made me a hero.

But then, you wouldn't be reading these words right now because the accident would have never happened. The point is, there are heroes everywhere, working every day, you just never hear about them. Why? Because they do things the right way the first time. They avoid accidents, risk, and danger in the first place. And that's the kind of quiet, routine, even boring heroism I want for you.

Take the time to think it through. Before you do something unsafe, on or off the job, just give yourself thirty seconds and do it the right way, the safe way. Don't go out in a blaze of glory like I almost did. Be a hero to your wife, your kids, your family, and your friends by living to spend another day with them. That's the kind of hero they want.

You know the best kind of hero? The best kind of hero doesn't wear a cape or drive a Batmobile or even fly. The best type of hero is careful, methodical, calm, cool, and collected. The best type of hero knows the value of his life and everyone around him.

In short, the best kind of hero is the one who's there, day in and day out, for his wife and his kids. The best kind of hero is the one who comes home, safe and sound, from a job that may be dangerous or may just be boring. It may not be sexy, but it's the best gift you can give yourself, your kids, your family, and your friends.

Parting Words about Safety on the Job: Sins of the Father

Listen, don't let my anger over carelessness and my passion for safety fool you; life is a blessing. Every day is a gift, and every sunset is a miracle. It's a shame that only those who have been so close to death fully realize how precious life really is.

I am constantly amazed by the miraculous, surprising, and blessed way my life is unfolding, even now. If you had told me years ago, in my alcoholic stupor or screaming in a debriding tank, that I would one day traipse around a crowded theme park—and happily so—with mouse ears on my head and wait forty-five minutes to get Donald Duck's autograph, I would have thought you were speaking Martian.

I have a beautiful granddaughter now. Her name is Jenny. All the time I robbed from her mother, I'm determined to pour into Jenny's life. The same way my father tried to spoil my brother and me, the same way I tried to spoil my daughters before the accident, I'm trying to spoil Jenny now.

When she was around seven, all Jenny wanted to do was go to Disney World. I would have taken her anywhere at that point—Hawaii, New York, LA—but all Jenny wanted was to go to Disney World. And so we did.

The plans this girl made. I've seen presidential campaigns less detail oriented. By the time we got to Orlando she had worked out an itinerary so complex I thought we might have to extend our vacation by a week to fit everything in.

It's a Small World. Dumbo. Buzz Lightyear. Splash Mountain. By the time we checked into the hotel, I knew everything the guidebooks had to say about these rides and dozens of others. And then Jenny saw it—the slide at the hotel pool.

Everything else was forgotten; forget Mickey Mouse, forget Minnie, forget Pluto and Donald and Tigger and Pooh. Jenny spent most of her vacation racing down the slide in the hotel pool.

Months of planning, gallons of highlighter ink spilled on exactly which rides she wanted to see and in which order, hundreds of dollars in theme park tickets, and Jenny's favorite part of Disney was the hotel pool.

I was waterlogged after the first day, and we still had a week left! The time in the sun was good for me. You see, nearly thirty years after my accident I'd just come off of my latest surgery. This one was too free up some mobility at my shoulder, and it was my sixth surgery of that year.

It was hard to believe that two and a half decades after nearly killing myself, I was still in therapy. But there it was. The surgery was behind me, and now I could relax with my family and little Jenny in the hotel pool.

Every time Jenny went down the slide, someone needed to be there waiting for her. Like I said, she was about seven at the time. And no matter who was there waiting for her at the bottom, smile wide, arms outstretched, Jenny would giggle and scream, "Catch me, Grandpa! Catch me!"

But I couldn't catch her. I couldn't be there to catch my granddaughter and swing her around the kiddie pool like the other grandfathers because twenty-five years earlier I'd taken one risk too many and I was still dealing with the fallout. I was still having surgeries to correct the mistakes I'd made three decades earlier.

And so as much as I wanted to spoil Jenny, as much as I wanted to undo the damage I'd done to her mother, as much as I'd promised Jenny I'd be there for her, there were still things I couldn't do for her because of my accident.

In the movies, things happen quickly. In the course of

two hours, the hero is introduced, faces a crisis, finds the resources he needs to solve it, goes through some ups and downs, and good or bad, reaches a conclusion. It may be a happy ending, it may be a sad one, and it may even lead to a sequel or a series, but whatever way, everything happens quickly.

In *Rocky*, you find out who wins the fight before the credits roll. Even if he loses, you find that out, too. There are no loose ends; everything's all neat and tidy as you walk out of the theater. Real life isn't so simple. To think that I'd still be dealing with the fallout from my accident thirty years later boggles my mind, but in many ways it also seems fitting.

I mean, why should life be easy? Why should I get off scot-free after what I'd done? And I'm fine with that; I'll take the heat. After this long, I know I can handle it. But it's my family I worry about. How long will my daughter have to make excuses for her old man? How long until I can be there at the bottom of the slide to catch my granddaughter?

How long will my family suffer for the sins of their father?

CHAPTER 12

The Phoenix Rises

At my seminars, during the question-and-answer period that follows, someone almost always asks me this question: "Charlie, we've heard about your past, we've heard about your accident, but...what's your life like today?"

This is one question I love to answer. Today I live the most exciting, adventurous, appreciative life you can imagine. And I'm not just talking about the places I get to go, the wonderful people I get to meet when I arrive, and the rewarding relationships my job has given me.

I'm talking about my priorities today. When you almost die, when you are literally brought back to life by the best doctors money can buy, your priorities change overnight.

What used to be important to me—the bills, the stress, the corporate ladder, the money, and the strife—all melted away. Not overnight maybe, but as my body healed, so did my soul.

Today all I need is a sunset and a smile and I'm a happy man. Of course, I don't stop there. I can vividly remember lying there on my deathbed in the hospital that first night. Couldn't feel a thing yet, couldn't speak, but I could tell I was dying. I could feel the life draining out of me, and I was too tired—body and soul—to fight it anymore.

I knew without a doubt I was going to die. I was ready for it, prepared to leave everything behind because the pain was just too great to live through. And as the monitors grew quiet, as the light dimmed, as the very hospital room seemed to disappear, I lay there thinking of all the things I never got to do: the mountains I hadn't climbed, the trips I hadn't taken, the places I hadn't seen, but more importantly, the things I hadn't said to my family, the time we hadn't spent with one another.

I was going to die the poorest kind of man, a man full of regret. But I didn't die. The doctors saved me, and while for many hard, agonizing, painful years I cursed them for doing so, in later years I thanked them profusely.

I knew I owed them a debt of gratitude because now I've been given a second chance at life. And I wasn't going to screw it up. I had a life to live, a family to embrace, and a future to look forward to, and I was going to appreciate and fully live every single moment.

But my life and my satisfaction and my joy are only part of the story. Because what waited for me around the corner was something more magical and eventful than I could have ever imagined.

And it all started with letting go, finally and at long last, of the blame and shame and guilt and anger that had dogged me through so much of my life. And I have a guy named Eddie to thank for that.

Thanks, Eddie

The first time I ever told my story, the real, honest to goodness, no BS, not edited for public consumption version of my accident, I wasn't onstage. I wasn't being filmed for one of my company's safety videos. I was yelling at some of my guys after being made safety supervisor at Exxon.

Now, the movie version was that I would have come back to work after my accident, scars all healed, grateful for the work, revved up with fire and brimstone, and ready to do God's work among the common man.

Well, not exactly. Instead I came back to Exxon the world's biggest victim. I was angry with everybody—with Exxon, with God, with my family, with my friends, and with my employees. Why? Because I blamed everybody and anybody for what had happened to me.

I was the world's biggest "Why me?" guy. And there I was, responsible for safety at the refinery I'd nearly blown to smithereens. And man, was my attitude rotten. In addition to feeling like the world's biggest victim, I also felt like the world's biggest babysitter.

All I did all day long was walk around, yelling at guys to put their helmets on, get their safety glasses off from the top of their heads, wear their fire-retardant clothing—all the things my safety manager used to yell at me before the accident.

And nobody listened; nobody cared. That's because they knew I didn't care. My guys could sense that I was there just to fill my days, punch in, punch out, and get to the nearest bar.

And man, were they ever right. Then one day I approached three guys I'd been yelling at all week. As they walked by, hats in hands, in an obvious danger zone, I lost it. I yelled at them, I cursed at them, I threatened them and told them to put their hats back on.

They walked away hatless. Finally, one of the guys turned around and said, "Charlie, you're full of it. You didn't care before the accident, and you don't care now. Why don't you just give it a rest?"

I lost it, again. I told those three guys, "Sit down!"

Amazingly, they did. And if you know Teamsters like I know Teamsters, then you'll spot this for the miracle it really is because Teamsters never do what you tell them to do.

Well, I started talking, and before I knew it, I was telling them my story—the story. The story you've just heard about the accident, the fire, the shower, the truck, the ambulance, my mother, my father, my wife and my kids, the scars and the operations, and the burns and the healing, and the drinking and the drugs, all of it uncensored, no BS.

It was the first time I'd ever told the whole story, and I don't know why it ever poured out of me that day, for that audience, at that moment. Perhaps it was God's way of relieving me of that burden, that heavy burden of guilt, of shame, or responsibility and misery I'd been dragging around ever since it happened.

Because suddenly, it felt as if a weight had been lifted off my shoulders. I know that sounds corny, but I could literally feel my posture straightening after years of guilt were released with every single word.

When I was done, those guys stood up, and one by one, they put their hats on. It wasn't a symbolic gesture, either. I never had to bark or yell at those three again. And as they were walking away, one of them turned around and gave me a chagrined smile.

I'll never forget it; his name was Eddie. I was loaded for bear, figuring he was about to give me some more business. Instead, Eddie smiled and said, "Jeez, Charlie, that was one great story; you should tell it to everyone…"

And I have been ever since.

A Dance with Destiny

Of course, I didn't throw off my tool belt and throw down my clipboard and tell my boss to "Take this job and shove it" the same day Eddie told me I should start telling my story to everyone. It was, as you might imagine, slightly more complicated than that.

The fact is, it wasn't just Eddie who convinced me that my story needed to be heard. After my first wife and I got divorced, I threw myself into my work, into my relationship with my daughters and their lives, and into my recovery.

I worked hard to give my daughters the life they deserved and to make up for the man that I'd been. But I had needs as well. After divorcing their mother, I was lonely for adult companionship. It's funny how when you stop drinking, your friends change. Or maybe not your friends so much, but certainly your routine.

For so many years, my routine had been to join my friends at the bar, with or without a wife. Now I worked and came home, living the straight life. My daughters were older now; they had lives of their own. And their old man? Well, he could have used a friend.

I found her at a singles dance. You believe that? Cool Charlie at a singles dance? I hadn't planned on going, not really. It was Thanksgiving weekend, and I was driving home from my brother's house after celebrating with him and his family.

There was a singles dance in a town called Spring Lake, New Jersey, and as I passed the community center there and saw the sign, I figured, *Why not?* It was either that or another lonely night at home.

Janet was the first woman I saw that night. She was beautiful—petite, dark hair, regal, and sophisticated. I knew I had to dance with her. Then again, without a few shots of courage in me, the old insecurities flared up. I said to myself, *Charlie, you ask that beautiful woman to dance, and if she says "yes," you'll stay. If she says "no," you're out of here!*

I introduced myself and asked her to dance. She hesitated; that was her way. Finally, she said "yes." That was it, I was staying. And if I was staying, I was determined to make the night worth my while.

Janet danced beautifully, but more than that, she was a wonderful listener. She was a teacher in the New York public school system and had a crack sense of humor and told great stories.

I asked her out on the spot. As she likes to tell the story, I asked her out for the next ten nights in a row.

"How about dinner tomorrow night?"

"There's a circus in town; how about going with me?"

All like that. I asked her to marry me the same way, time and time again. We dated for two years before she finally said "yes." But I'd convinced myself nearly a year earlier that Janet would be the woman I'd marry.

We were on a trip to the city and it was wintertime. Janet saw a homeless guy on the street, while it was snowing, no socks on his feet. We had plans for all kinds of things, city plans, but nothing would do but for Janet to go from store to store trying to find socks for this man. When she finally found some, she returned humbly and handed them to him—no fanfare, no glory, just mission accomplished, and now we could go on with our evening.

I knew right then, she was the woman for me. And her? Well, she just needed a little convincing, that's all. But she finally gave in. Cool Charlie, he wore her down.

Actually, I tell everyone that Janet would have never married the guy I was, only the guy she helped me become.

And she wasn't content with turning me into a great husband; she had much more in store for me. In fact, it was Janet who convinced me to go into business for myself.

You see, I met Janet at a crossroads in my life. I was working at Exxon, and she was a teacher. We fell in love and got married. We both had day jobs—me as safety manager, she in education. We did fine, we were happy with each other, but she felt I had more to offer.

And me? Well, I still had Eddie's words ringing in my ears: "Jeez, Charlie, that was one great story; you should tell it to everyone…" I started thinking about what he had said and what it might mean for my life. Eddie was right; more people needed to hear my story and more than just the guys at the plant. (Who, frankly, were tiring of the story!)

When I shared Eddie's story with Janet, she hopped right on it. I mean, she wouldn't let up. This amazing woman, she was absolutely for it. We started small; we started familiar: with Exxon.

It was strictly part-time at first. A weekend seminar here, a safety meeting with a few line guys here, a coffee klatch meet and greet with some supervisors there.

I learned I had a passion for and a natural talent for speaking to people. Not because I was glib or polished, but because I cared about the message and the people so much. Janet was great. If I came home feeling I hadn't done enough or the meeting ran too short or groaning "I should have said this, I should have said that," she'd help me finesse the message, help me go over my lines.

She picked out my clothes for me, helped me negotiate fees.

Fees? Can you imagine, getting paid to do what you'd do for free? What you're passionate about? What you care about the most? But it was expensive, taking time off from work and traveling here, traveling there.

She worked out a fee structure, helped me bill for expenses, showed me that I would never be in business until I started treating what I did like a business.

One presentation led to two. I began traveling more to reach a wider audience. Exxon would send me here, send me there. Apparently, there was a big market for safety and not a lot of speakers to fill it.

With each presentation, my story solidified. It came back to me, in shimmering detail or flashes of crystal clear memory; not all of the memories were welcome, but all made it into my presentation. And people responded. They wanted more. More of my story and how it could be applied to their lives.

They were hungry for safety, tired of the dull routine and the risks involved in their jobs. If I had managed to do anything unique with my story, it was to make it personal for them, to give safety and hazard and risk a face.

I was away from work more and more. Sadly, I was away from home more and more as well. I missed my wife and wanted her to join me on my travels. But we both had full-time jobs.

Then Janet made a startling suggestion. She wanted me to quit my job at Exxon and speak full-time. My initial reaction was shock, then fear. "What? Janet, I'm almost fifty. Starting over is for young guys. I can't do this; it will never work…"

But much as I'd pursued her hand in marriage, Janet was like a dog with a bone; she just wouldn't give up on the idea. She made me believe in myself, in my story, and in turning a dream into reality. Eventually, I started to think about it more in terms of reality than fantasy.

Start life over? Really? Start a company that specialized in going around to all these other companies, speaking about safety? Seriously? Could it work? *Would* it work? I started checking around, doing some research. Other people had actually done it. Maybe not in safety per se, but in other specialized industries.

In fact, I suddenly remembered a man named Jack Ware. Jack was a former state trooper who was so passionate about seat belt safety that he made it his life's work to educate safe drivers all over the country. He produced a series of videos called Room to Live.

I remember going to see Jack Ware when I worked at Exxon, long after the accident. He gave a powerful presentation about children dying in seat belts. I was so moved, the moment stuck with me, and after a life lived virtually seat belt free, I've been wearing my seat belt ever since.

So I knew it was possible. I knew this could happen, but I was still hesitant. I mean, when you're in your golden years, the last thing you want is to start over, and essentially, that's what we'd be doing. No, not essentially, that's *exactly* what we'd be doing.

We were comfortable in our lives, but we did it anyway. We started a company, Phoenix Safety Management, Inc. The name fit. I truly felt like a phoenix who'd been born again, rising from the fire to live another day and never looking back at the life he left behind. The company became official. Phoenix Safety Management, Inc. was in business.

And now I've written this book to share my story and what I've learned. For better or worse, Charlie's story is now public property.

I don't mind; I'm proud of the man I am now. I couldn't always say that. I'm proud because now rather than hating my life, I'm living it. I'm enjoying it. What's more, rather than training guys to do things the wrong way, I'm part of a new generation of safety professionals training them to do things the right way, the safe way.

And as far as I'm concerned, if I can save one person's life, all the scars, all the pain, all the tears, all the drama will have been worth it.

It happens, every once in a while. Awhile back I was speaking out in Utah, at one of the mines there. And before I spoke to the second shift, one of the miners who had heard me speak earlier in the day came up to me. And very hesitantly, he asked me, "Charlie, is it okay if I bring my son back to hear you speak tonight? He's fourteen years old and just got a dirt bike, but for the life of me I can't get him to wear his helmet. I think you might be able to help."

I said, "Sure, no problem. Always happy to help if I can..."

Sure enough, after my talk to the second shift, a shy, unassuming boy came up to thank me for letting him come. I smiled and shook his hand, and he quickly said his good-byes.

I didn't think much of it until a few months later when I was back at the same plant, giving another speech. Almost immediately, the same miner came up to me, and the man was crying profusely. His face was black with coal, and there were actually streaks from the tears. I'll never forget it.

I didn't know what to think. Had I upset him in some way? Then the miner told me why he was crying. He said a little while back, his son had been in a major motocross accident. He'd flipped the bike, came down on his head, broken his collarbone, but he survived because he had his helmet on.

The man said, "Charlie, I want to thank you for saving my son's life." What do you do after someone tells you something like that? Other than walk around on cloud nine for a while I mean? That's the kind of thing I live for now.

That's the kind of thing that, frankly, makes life worth living.

Epilogue

Meet Rosie the elephant! Isn't she beautiful? She's the newest member of the Morecraft family.

Much as I never set out to become a safety consultant, speak around the world on safety, or even write a book about it, I never set out to "adopt" an elephant, either.

Then a funny thing happened on the way to my future. A veterinarian I've been taking my pets to for years, a man by the name of Jim Laurita, called me up one day. Now, Jim is an interesting guy. You know how kids always say they want to run away and join the circus? Well, Jim did it.

He actually dropped out of college and joined the circus. Eventually, Jim got promoted from juggler to ring announcer to...elephant trainer. He eventually went on to become a veterinarian, but his passion remained with circus animals.

And here's where I come in. Jim called me on the phone and said there was this elephant, Rosie, who was in bad shape. She lived with lots of other bigger elephants at a circus in Oklahoma. The other elephants picked on her, she'd been injured, and she had arthritis.

As Jim talked, I wondered where this was going. (Although I must confess, I kind of already knew.) Finally, Jim said he was trying to bring Rosie back to Maine, where we both lived, so he could take care of her full-time.

"Obviously," Jim said, finally getting to the punch line, "it costs a lot of money to transport an elephant across the country. Would you like to help?"

I knew Jim. I trusted Jim. But I like to see where my money is going. Besides, who doesn't want to run away to the circus at least once in his life? (Even if it's just for a visit?) I said, "Jim, I'll help you, but I want to see Rosie first."

Jim didn't flinch. He knew I was already hooked, and he was just waiting to see how big a fish he'd caught. We immediately flew out to Oklahoma, where I met Rosie for the first time. Not surprisingly, I fell in love and wrote Jim a check for $15,000 on the spot.

Back home in the tiny town of Hope, Maine—fitting, isn't it?—Jim and a dedicated team of elephant experts are preparing for the day when Rosie will finally make the trip to her new home.

It hasn't been easy, and it hasn't been cheap. We're helping Jim build a huge barn for Rosie to live in, complete with a heated floor and a pool like you wouldn't believe. The pool is designed to help rehab Rosie's legs, with a treadmill on the bottom and powerful jets for her aqua therapy.

And since elephants don't like to live in isolation, she'll have a goat as a companion for a year, after which Jim hopes to bring in another elephant to keep Rosie company.

The King of Second Chances

I can't help but see parallels between Rosie's story and my own. I was fortunate enough to be able to give Rosie a second chance, a fresh start on life. This coming from me, the King of Second Chances.

Life has hurt Rosie; she's been beaten down and abused and needed someone to help her through life's roughest patch. I wouldn't be here now if it hadn't been for the forgiveness, the grace, the kindness of my family, of my co-workers, of my bosses, of the folks at Exxon, and everyone who's ever heard me speak.

Rosie and I, it seems, we're two of a kind. And I'm proud to be her adoptive "uncle" for however long she'll let me be. But I also know, as any uncle knows, that after all the love and tenderness, after all the special care and the rehab, like me, she'll have to stand on her own someday.

Like any child, Rosie is only on loan to our family. One day, she'll need to be free and live life on her own four feet. I, too, had to find my own way in this life. The folks who carried me for years could only carry me so long or so far. I only hope that Rosie can find the same kind of happiness in her future as I've found in mine.

I feel a special bond with Rosie. I feel protective of her. When I was injured, when I was sick and in pain, I had a voice. I could say, "I hurt here," and someone would come tend to me. Rosie has no voice. She's an animal, and I'm proud to be involved, in whatever way I can, in giving her a great, big, fat second chance.

And what now? Here we are at the end of our journey. I hope you've learned a lot about safety, about yourself, about others, and about personal responsibility. I say learned, but really, you probably knew all that already. I should say I hope I've reminded you about all those things. That's really what I do; I'm a reminder.

- A reminder of the risks involved in industrial plants
- A reminder of what can happen if you're not careful
- A reminder of what skirting safety protocol can do to you
- A reminder of redemption
- A reminder of life's great second chances

- A reminder, finally, of how beautiful life can be if only we'll look up from our lives now and again and appreciate it...

At work or at home, safety is a joint effort. If you see someone getting ready to make a big mistake, I hope by now I've given you the tools and the confidence to stop them with a gentle, personal reminder: "I care about you; I care about your eyes, your fingers, your toes. Do this the right way. Go home and hug your kids tonight..."

But if you ever need a reminder or just a refresher course or simply a question answered or a concern raised, I'm always here for you. That's what I do, remember? I'm a reminder, and I'm always around. Just pop into my website at www.charliemorecraft.com and let me know what's on your mind.

Rosie and I will be waiting for you...

about the author

CHARLIE MORECRAFT

As an oil refinery employee, Charlie considered himself one of the guys, and his company and union considered him a good worker. With fifteen years of experience, he knew all the safety procedures—and how to get around them. In 1980, shortcuts nearly cost him his life when a routine job turned tragic.

Burned over 50 percent of his body, Charlie spent five years in the hospital. His family fell apart. He lost everything. "All for what?" is the question he continues to ask himself and you today. Charlie, a dynamic speaker who touches an audience through his autobiographical story, emphasizes taking responsibility for one's actions and one's safety. Standard training meetings, videos, and seminars demonstrate *how* to follow safety procedures. Charlie Morecraft tells you *why* you should.